Daybreak

Daybreak

52 Things Nature Teaches Us

Lessons for Seeking
the Natural Element in Everyday Life

Amy E. Dean

With photographs from
the American Museum of Natural History

M. Evans and Company, Inc.
New York

M. Evans and Company, Inc.
216 East 49th Street
New York, New York 10017

Library of Congress Cataloging-in-Publication Data

Dean, Amy
  Daybreak : 52 things nature teaches us : lessons for seeking
the natural element in everyday life / Amy E. Dean. — 1st ed.
    p.   cm.
  ISBN 0-87131-808-3 (hardcover). — ISBN 0-87131-811-3
(6-copy prepack)
  1. Philosophy of nature.   I. Title.
BD581.D277   1996
113—dc20   96-19225
                                                CIP

Book design by Annemarie Redmond

Manufactured in the United States of America

First Edition

9 8 7 6 5 4 3 2 1

To my parents who put labels on all of my summer clothes, packed them into an ugly metal trunk, rolled up a sleeping bag, slipped batteries into a flashlight, loaded me down with bug repellent, and sent me off to camp for the summer.

I thought I would never come back alive.

But when they came to take me home, I didn't want to leave. So I dedicate this book to my parents, who gave me a most incredible and everlasting gift — an enduring love for nature.

Thanks, Mom and Dad, for my summers
at Camp Wampatuck.

Introduction

Greek Stoic philosopher Zeno once advised that "The goal of life is living in agreement with Nature." Throughout the history of the world, humankind has proudly displayed this ability to live life agreeably with nonhumankind. Prehistoric ancestors honored the living things with whom they shared their environment with cave paintings. The ancient Egyptians, Greeks, and Romans created and worshipped gods and goddesses that personified nature and explained nature's mysteries to them. Religious leaders sought answers to life and drew closer to God by studying birds, stars, and flowers. Poets composed odes to the beauty of nature. Philosophers and scientists valued the naturalistic viewpoint in their studies. American Indian tribes believed that all wisdom and knowledge were with the animals and, according to Pawnee Eagle Chief (Letakots-Lesa), "The One Above...sent certain animals to tell men that he showed himself through the beasts, and that from them, and from the stars and the sun and the moon should man learn."

In the mid-nineteenth century, observation of nature rose to an all-time high. Theodore Roosevelt and William Beebe traveled to exotic locales and wrote about their exciting adventures. "The Golden Age of Nature Writing" featured naturalists such as John Muir, John Burroughs, W. H. Hudson, and Henry David Thoreau, who recorded their own first-hand experiences with nature. Thousands of years after Zeno's death in 263 B.C., Thoreau echoed the Greek's advice by writing, "Think of our life in nature, — daily to be shown matter, to come in contact with it, — rocks, trees, wind on our cheeks! the *solid* earth! the *actual* world! the *common sense! Contact! Contact! Who* are we? *Where* are we?"

Nature is as much a physical entity as it is a social one; in addition to the resources it provides for itself — for self-preservation — as well as for humankind — for enjoyment, use, and, oftentimes, abuse — nature plays an important role in the daily life of human society. Although there will always be a fundamental distinction between humans and nature and even though nature, by at least one definition, is anything not modified or created by man, nature does have a relationship with humanity. Too, humanity has a relationship with nature. Nature is the starting point of all living things as well as their sustainer. Nature, therefore, is essential to humankind; referring to nature as "Mother Nature" is apt, for nature is humankind's nurturing protector.

In today's society, however, Mother Nature has been left with many empty nests. For as most people grow older, they come to believe that nature isn't "where it's at." Where it's at, they discover, is in the city, in front of the computer, in the living room watching television, on the telephone, in the midst of a morning or evening commute, in the middle of a project, in the throes of trying to balance a full-time job with part-time night school, in the day-to-day stresses of being a single parent — in sum, in countless other pursuits, problems, and pastimes.

If you're like most people, you may find it hard — if not impossible — to sustain the joy and wonder you experienced from nature when you were a child. "In this modern age," comments an unknown source, "very little remains that is real. Night has been banished, so have the cold, the wind, and the stars. They have all been neutralized; the rhythm of life obscured. Everything goes so fast and makes so much noise, and men hurry by without heeding the grass by the roadside, its color, its smell and the way it shimmers when the wind caresses it." Yet it is in the experience of nature that you can truly find yourself, for nature can teach you about your strengths, how to trust, what the answers are as well as what questions should be asked, how life and death must walk hand in hand, about silences and nothingness, about floundering and discovery, about patience and hope, about magic and wonder, about the difference between loneliness and solitude, and many other valuable lessons.

This book reminds you of some of nature's lessons that you may have forgotten over the years or have become too busy to pay attention to in the hustle and bustle of your everyday life. They are lessons that can never be learned from books, from experts, or from the media. They are lessons that come from the fields, the sky, the woods, the river bank, the seashore, the animals, the earth. And they are lessons delivered by teachers that "...have been the birds themselves...the sun when it left a glow of crimson behind it at setting, the very trees, and wild herbs."

Nature's lessons can make valuable contributions to your life. Take time to read them, think about them, and learn from them. By seeking the natural elements in your everyday life, you can strengthen your relationship with nature and, in so doing, improve the quality of your life.

Imagination

*"Worlds can be found by a child and an adult
bending down and looking together under the grass stems
or at the skittering crabs in a tidal pool."*

— American anthropologist Mary Catherine Bateson

"Never in my wildest imagination did I ever think..." might be how you'd begin a story about a job promotion you had just received, a degree you had just earned, a dream house you had just purchased, a new love interest you had just met. There may be many other achievements in your life that you once had thought might never come true. But did you ever really *imagine* that they'd never come true? More likely than not such things had been part of your active imagination for a long time; you had probably visualized they would happen and then not only hoped they would, but expended time and energy to ensure they could. So your wildest dreams *did* eventually come true, with help from your determination, your capabilities, a bit of good luck, and your imagination.

Imagination is seeing or believing something meaningful where none currently exists. So imagination can be lying on your back and staring up at the clouds in the sky and seeing, from the scattered cirrus and cumulus conglomerations of floating water vapor, horses stampeding across the prairie and a New York City skyscraper and Abraham Lincoln's face. Imagination can be looking at a crackling fire and seeing, in the glowing red and orange embers and flickering yellow flames, firebreathing dragons and jungle animals looking back at you. Imagination can be digging your fingers deep into a sandy beach and fashioning a castle from tiny grains of sand, constructing a moat around the castle, decorating turrets with bright candy wrappers, and creating a fairy-tale land of kings and queens and knights in shining armor.

As well, imagination can be watching the birds soar in the sky and thinking, "I can do that," and then constructing replicas of wings to attach to your arms, walking to the top of a hill, and then racing down, flapping your winged arms and leaping into the air. Imagination makes all things probable and, in many cases, possible. Each day, thousands of humanity's winged birds take flight, all because someone once saw birds soaring overhead and asked, "What if?" Walk down any city sidewalk, and you'll see examples of how the human mind has used imagination to translate what exists in nature for its own purposes. Threads of telephone wires drape from location to location — connecting strands in an intricate web that allows you to communicate with others and to receive communication, much as the delicate strands on a spider's web signal the tiny

weaver. Streams of people flow in and out of the ground like busy ants as they tunnel from one location to another on subway systems. People bustle about, communicating with one another often times without sound, using instead body posturing, hand and arm motions, head nods, smiles and frowns, much as animals communicate with one another.

When Orson Welles broadcast his famous *The War of the Worlds,* he could never have imagined that his listeners would have believed that an invasion by Martians was imminent. But the planet that is over forty-million miles from Earth had already been brought into bedrooms and living rooms with the creation of the telescope. Even though the American space program was decades away, the possibility of space flight and the creation of spaceships had already been instilled in the imaginations of many. So all Orson Welles did was what H. G. Wells had done when he first wrote the story, *The War of the Worlds;* he made dragons in a fire and wild horses in clouds. He used his imagination.

Imagination is also evidence of thinking, of being able to resolve conflicts and to seek solutions to perplexing problems. For many, this inspiration has come from nature. For example, Newton's laws of gravity came from observing an apple fall from the tree to the ground, and the design of military combat uniforms is based on the survival camouflage of creatures in their environments.

Too, imagination is the unending ability to wonder — to be continually astonished by the world around you. For many, this sense of wonder may have ended in childhood at about the same time learning focused on the memorization of facts such as the year Christopher Columbus set sail, the capital of North Dakota, and the number of acres in a square mile. But this sense of wonder — this ability to appreciate the world around you, to treat it with awe and curiosity, to approach new things willingly and with a sense of innocence — can be restored at any age. All you have to do is stop and notice phenomena in the world around you. Pick up a rock from the ground and feel its texture, the solidness of its form. Bend down next to your sleeping dog and listen to the gentle rhythm of the rise and fall of its breath. Grow an avocado tree from the pit. Borrow a stethoscope and listen to the sound of your own heartbeat.

Begin today to look under grass stems and at the skittering crabs in tidal pools on the beach so you can learn to look at life, your environment, and the universe as if for the first time, without preconceptions, without searching for quick answers, and with a willingness to discover as much as you can from what you see. Exercise your imagination every day in this way, and you'll develop a sense of wonder that will be, as environmentalist and marine biologist Rachel Carson determined, "so indestructible that it would last a lifetime, as an unfailing antidote against the boredom and disenchantments of later years, the sterile preoccupation with things that are artificial, the alienation from the sources of [y]our strength."

Power

"We should be as water,
which is lower than all things yet stronger
even than the rocks."

— Oglala Sioux proverb

Go for a walk on a rainy day, and you'll know how brooks, creeks, and rivers are formed. The tiny rivulets you see at your feet run quickly by on their way to a newly formed stream; it takes hundreds of them to make a brook, hundreds more to create a creek, hundreds times hundreds more to flow as a river.

Even the tiniest drops of rain have the power to stream down city streets, rapidly fill depressions on a road or sidewalk, surge into storm sewers, urge leaves, sticks, and other debris along with them — all on a merry romp. Sometimes the romp can get so rambunctious or go on for so long that basements flood, seashores erode, roads close, people and animals perish. All these things can result from a single drop of rain. Raindrops combined with other raindrops over a period of time have the power to flood and destroy; too, such rain has the power to quench and nourish.

For as technologically advanced as the civilization in which you're living is, nature is still all-powerful. Rain can destroy a farmer's business as well as make it flourish. Snow can bring a metropolis to its knees as well as create recreational activities for millions. Wind can knock down power lines as well as effortlessly dry loads of laundry without the use of gas or electricity. Sunshine can scorch the earth as well as ripen fruits and vegetables. Storms can disrupt schedules, create foul tempers, and challenge many "indestructible" inventions of a civilization that considers it vital to categorize natural elements over which it has no control as either good or bad. However, nature — like weather — just is; as well, nature's power just is.

One of the most important lessons that can be learned from nature is in its power. You might view this power as controlling, particularly when it's your weekend golf game that's been canceled because of rain or your bad back that suffers after shoveling out from yet another record snowfall. Yet somewhere a garden is being watered while you're fretting and fuming about your missed golf game and somewhere else a family is joyously building snowcaves together in the high snowbanks while you're icing your back. Nature ministers to all; it's your interpretation of nature's ministry that determines how you view as well as how you accept nature's power.

Naturalist Henry David Thoreau, who lived close to nature and was able to view nature's power with patience and detachment, once watched the spring rain from his cabin window at Walden Pond and wrote: "The gentle rain which waters my beans and keeps me in the house today is not drear and melancholy, but good for me too. Though it prevents my hoeing them, it is of far more worth than my hoeing. If it should continue so long as to cause the seeds to rot in the ground and destroy the potatoes in the low lands, it would still be good for the grass on the uplands, and being good for the grass, it would be good for me." But how often do you view natural occurrences with the same objective eye, as neither good nor bad, but worthwhile in some way?

Too often you may equate the term power with that which controls or manipulates you. So that means government is power. Church is power. Corporations are power. Your doctor is power. Your boss is power. Your life partner is power. Your children are power. Your parents are power. As a result, you may hate power, fear power, run from power, and rebel against power.

But do small craft warnings posted on a windy day that prevent you from a Sunday boating outing have this same power over you? Is a tree that has rotted and fallen across a mountain path, diverting you and your mountain bike from your usual route, have this same power over you? Does an endangered species that diverts or delays construction because of where it nests have this same power over you?

In nature, there's an important difference between power and strength. Nature is not "out for itself"; it has no agenda and no personal vendetta against you or anyone else. Nature, like you, is part of an infinitely larger whole and, like you, progresses through its own slowly evolving cycles of change and growth. Any disruption it may cause in one area, such as by a flood or an earthquake, often has the opposite effect in another area. But unlike you, nature seeks to establish harmony and balance, and such things are not the components of a power that manipulates or controls.

The parable about the bet the wind made with the sun provides a good example of the difference between nature's power and the power that has been created by human nature. The wind bet the sun that it could make a man who was walking along the road remove his jacket. So the wind blew furiously at and around the man, frantic to prove itself right and win the bet. But the man only pulled his coat tighter around him. Then the sun took its turn. The sun gently beat its warm rays down on the man and soon the man willingly removed his coat. Such is the simple strength of nature. Such also is the lesson of nature's power. Nature gives life to the world as well as takes it away. Natures shapes all things, sometimes breaking them down and sometimes building them up. Nature nurtures and supports growth through cycles that include life as well as death. And nature serves as your teacher and guide for the limited time you have on Earth.

When you can honor nature's power — knowing that you can never possess or control it but that from it you can attain infinite wisdom — then you'll be able to appreciate that each rainy day creates a stream that is a novelty, something that will be gone at the end of the storm to make way for something new.

Love

"...there is indeed a chasm which separates man and animal, and...if that chasm is to be bridged, it must be man who does it by means of understanding. But before we can understand, we must know; and to know, we must love. We must love life in all its forms, even in those which we find least attractive."

— French marine explorer Jacques-Yves Cousteau

In the 1950s the World Health Organization tried to eliminate malaria in northern Borneo by using the pesticide dieldrin to kill mosquitoes that were carrying the disease. Almost immediately, the project appeared to be a success. The mosquitoes disappeared; incidences of malaria dramatically decreased. But then something strange happened. The roofs of the villagers began falling in on them and the people faced the threat of a typhoid epidemic. Why? The thatched roofs collapsed because the dieldrin also killed the wasps and insects that ate the caterpillars that fed on the roofs; hundreds of lizards died from eating the poisoned mosquitoes; the village cats died from eating the poisoned lizards; and rats began to run rampant through the village, carrying typhus-infested fleas with them.

The moral of the story is, everything in life is interconnected; eliminating even one living thing can have detrimental effects and even larger implications upon others. To maintain the delicate balance of life, every living thing must be respected and embraced. So as annoying as mosquitoes are, eliminating them means upsetting other cycles of life; to be able to live with them then, despite their peskiness and disease-carrying abilities, ensures safeguarding the lives of other more beneficial living things.

So, too, it is with human love. If you were just to pick and choose a few select people to love — people to whom you would show compassion, passion, tenderness, acceptance, support, peace, harmony, honesty, trust, and openness — and then not love others, you would be eliminating other people from your life who might not only be vital to the balance of your life, but also to all of humanity. For the natural way of love is one that brings greater harmony not only to your world, but also to the world around you.

What good does love do when you hug and kiss your loved ones before you leave for work, and then scream at other drivers on the road on your commute, shove your way by others who are sharing the sidewalk with you, push your way into an already crowded elevator, snarl at your assistants, look with disdain at the panhandlers on your way to pick up a sandwich for lunch, step around an elderly person who is struggling with packages, work so that only you alone look good, gripe about how little you're getting paid for what you do, and then get back in your car to go home to hug and kiss your loved ones?

Taoist Chuang-Tzu taught that, "through love, we experience the inherent connections between ourselves and others, seeing all creation as one." But you can only experience love in this way when you're able to look beyond your ego and beyond individual personalities and passions to perceive your part in a much larger pattern — one that exists beyond heart and head. Love can unite you with the good of all and in all, but only if you're able to express love with no thought of return, transcend judgment and break the habit of analysis and comparison to others, release your anger — even in a hostile world — and seek outlets for harmonious and peaceful interactions, live completely in the present to avoid regret over the past and expectations for the future, and circulate loving energy to heal yourself and your world.

Denying love to strangers, to those who are less fortunate than you, to those who have hurt you in the past, to those who deny you love, to those who don't measure up to your standards, to those who have more than you do, or to those who discriminate against you fragments you as an individual and divides humanity. For, as

Diane Dreher, author of *The Tao of Inner Peace* suggests: "Imagine how much freer your relationships would be.... Imagine how the nations of this world would relate if they released the centuries of conflict, prejudice, and suspicion that divide them... they could work together to solve our global problems of hunger and pollution. Eliminating the blaming and posturing, they could get down to constructive action, building bridges of peace instead of walls of hostility."

To harmonize with yourself and the others in your world, you need to love every living thing. Certainly there will be mosquitos and many other living things you'll come in contact with that you may be hard pressed to love but, too, there will be many treasures — wonderful people, wonderful sunrises, wonderful wildflowers, wonderful wildlife — that touch your heart in very special, very loving ways. All must be loved in order for all to be united.

Wonder

"One vivid memory remains of passing through the city. A small boy, five or six at most, had picked up a dead monarch butterfly from a pile of litter beside the street. He was standing entranced, bending forward, oblivious to all around him. It seemed as though I were looking at myself when young. A door was opening for him, a door beyond which lay all the beauty and mystery of nature."

— American nature writer Edwin Way Teale

When was the last time you had a "close encounter" with the astonishing world around you? Because you may live in an apartment or home far away from natural surroundings such as the woods or the seashore, because you may have to work or study inside for long periods of time, or because an illness or disability may hinder your mobility, you may think that you can't experience the many wonders of the natural world.

But if, when standing on your balcony, gazing out of your bedroom window, or walking your dog, you look up at the night sky for a few minutes, you might be able to catch — for a split second — a shooting star. If, the next time you stroll through the city or walk across a field at dusk and notice a flock of starlings wheeling back and forth across the sky, you may be witnessing the roller-coaster antics of the members of an amazing aviarian family tree — descendants from the original group of eighty European starlings that Eugene Scheifflin, a bird watcher, introduced into New York City's Central Park in 1890. If, while sitting in your home or office, you spy a housefly hovering about, you can take time to marvel at its ability to land on the ceiling, walk upside down, and evade all of your subversive attempts to kill it.

You don't have to live in nature to be able to wonder at nature. You can start an herb garden from seeds in a sunny window, grow orchids in a warm room, or produce organic tomatoes in a rooftop garden. You can assemble a terrarium that houses hermit crabs, lizards, spiders, or snakes or an aquarium for freshwater or tropical fish. You can set up a telescope and observe the night sky or watch the life cycle of pigeons roosting on an opposite building ledge.

But you also don't have to exert any effort at all to encounter nature's marvels. Everyday wonders can be found all around you; like "purloined letters," they're always in full view — as obvious as can be — but only if you take the time to notice them. For example, gravity is a constant force in your life; without it, you and all of your possessions would be floating freely about. Every day, without realizing it, you breathe in and out about five hundred cubic feet of air; this air miraculously links you with every living thing as well as provides you with the essential respiration you need to ride a bike or write a memo. Every day the sun rises and sets; each day brings a new weather pattern; each day has the same period of time in it. Seasons change on cue, constellations revolve around the sky, tides ebb and flow.

All these things happen whether or not you notice them. But, when you take time to notice them, such events can become much more significant, much more wonderous. As American humorist Garrison Keillor once remarked, "Tiny white crystalline flakes falling through the air, billions of them which when you take some in your hand and study them, no two are the same. You can't study them long because they melt in your hand, but no two are the same, that's what they say. But who said this? Who would do a study of billions of snowflakes to prove no repetition?" Yet someone did take time to notice them — to wonder at them — just like the little boy took the time to reach into a pile of litter to extricate the delicate carcass of the monarch butterfly so he could study it.

Nature opens doors of wonder to everyone; it's up to you to step through them. Remember that each day you live out your life against a wonderful tapestry of astonishing phenomena. Start to wonder now, and you'll soon be entertained, stimulated, and enlightened by the world around you. Love to wonder, and your life can become a delightful adventure of discovery.

Sensuality

*"Hold out your hands
to feel the luxury of the sunbeams."*

— American writer and lecturer
Helen Keller

Even though Helen Keller was blind, deaf, and mute, she knew what a mountain lion looked like. She could describe its color, the texture of its fur, the feel of its twitching tail, the ferocity that burned in its eyes, the sharpness of its teeth, the sound of its snarl and purr, the firmness of the pads of its feet, the sharp prick and tear its claws could inflict upon its prey.

She knew all this from a mountain lion she examined at the hands-on museum at the Perkins School for the Blind in Watertown, Massachusetts. The 163-year-old Perkins' museum is unique not only because it's one of relatively few tactual museums in the country, but also because of its expansive collection, which presents items from the everyday world as well as more exotic species for the vision-impaired to hold and examine.

Teachers at the school find that just one touch can change confusion to clarity, for many of those who are vision-impaired have never seen everyday sights you may take for granted — a squirrel or blue jay, for instance, a daisy, a cloud in the sky, or a beam of sunlight. "Squirrels are all over the place," Paula Huffman, a science teacher at the school, says, "but how do you explain one to a blind child? [Or] take a blue jay. They are noisy and arrogant — but they are small birds. They just sound big." Teacher Marie Heaton adds, "The children are amazed by things we take for granted —

how big a turkey's tail is, a reindeer." One student learned that a rabbit's ears flopped but a penguin's didn't; another learned how to distinguish a squirrel from a cat; another found out that a fox wasn't waist-high after all. "I read about foxes and just thought they were bigger because of the way they were described in books," explained vision-impaired student Karen Nickerson. "I didn't know they were small until I felt one."

The subtlety of nature is sometimes greater than the subtlety of the senses; Helen Keller learned this by holding out her hands to feel a sunbeam or cupping them together to catch water gushing out from a pump. But to be able to distinguish nature's even more mysterious subleties — the delicacies of color hidden away in the chalice of a flower; the orchestral-like movement of a sea of grass as it shifts and bends in response to the wind, its invisible conductor; the lively sound of waves rolling pebbles, grains of sand, and shells on the shore as they drone on in incessant "wavespeak" to anyone who will listen; the earthy smells that invade the nostrils on the first warm day of spring and entice, provoke, excite, and lure — requires you to make the transition from sensory awareness to sensual abandonment.

Nature is a truly sensual, sensory experience. You can observe nature, you can study nature, you can discuss nature, but to truly experience it, you must abandon the intellect and savor the effect it creates — that of pure sensation. You can close your eyes and sense the colors of nature without seeing them. You can peer through binoculars at the lumbering gait of a porcupine and sense the stiffness of its quills without touching them. You can hold a seashell in your hand and sense the smell of the sea without inhaling it. You can see a flash of lightning off in the distance and sense the answering rumble of thunder without hearing it. You can peel an orange and sense its flavor without tasting it.

Nature teaches you much about sensuality. Nature implores you, "Please touch!" Nature invites you, "Please taste!" Nature beseeches you, "Please look!" Nature begs you, "Please listen!" Nature alerts you, "Please smell!" Nature tempts and teases you to hold and examine it, to bend down and put your nose in it, to call out to it and hear its reply, to touch it with your tongue or chew and swallow it, to leer at it and peer at it.

Nature can charge your senses as well as reach down into your soul and make you feel alive, joyful, dreamy, sad, reassured, and touch you in very special, very sensual ways.

Harmony

"When you know nature as part of yourself,
You will act in harmony.
When you feel yourself part of nature,
You will live in harmony."

— *Tao, 13*

When John Donne penned years ago that no man was an island, that each human being was "...a piece of the continent, a part of the main," he could have added that no part of nature was an island, that every living thing was a piece of humanity as well as a part of the main. Both man and nature are part of a much larger pattern, a pattern of harmony that intrinsically links them together in a dynamic web of life. This implies that any loss in nature is also a loss for humanity; therefore, man is not only integral, but also responsible for maintaining the harmony in nature.

To understand this principle of oneness, think about a loved one you may have lost from your life. Do you remember what your first holiday gathering after this loss was like? You may have felt a definite void, a sense that a vital piece of you and your family was missing, a feeling that the gathering was in some way imbalanced or "out of synch." Later on, there may have been a time when you had good news to share and, in your excitement, reached automatically for the phone to dial the once-familiar number before you stopped short with the recollection that this special person was no longer there. Once again, you may have felt your world disrupted, a pattern to which you had grown accustomed taken away from

you, leaving you with the feeling of not only having lost one beloved person, but also a bit of yourself as well.

Just as you may take for granted the harmony of your world until it's disrupted, so, too, you may take for granted the harmony of the natural world. You trust that the sun and moon will rise and set each day, the tide will ebb and flow, and the seasons will change as they always have. You don't get up every morning and worry whether the sun will rise or stand on a beach at low tide, concerned that the waves won't return to shore. Without your doing anything, much of the harmony of nature remains firmly in place.

But when man impacts upon nature — through pollution, defilement, squalor, and other forms of natural destruction — the harmony of nature as well as the harmony of humanity can be destroyed in ways that have an immediate as well as a lasting impact. Quite often this happens when man behaves as if he were an island, concerned only with his own welfare, incapable of seeing the much larger harmonious patterns he may be destroying.

For example, the coastal town of Pacific Grove in California has long been known for its monarch butterflies; in fact, so many people have come to Pacific Grove to see the return of the brilliant orange insects that the butterflies were elevated to the status of town symbol; their image was emblazoned street signs, maps, and promotional materials. But in the early 1990s there was a dramatic decrease in the butterflies because increased development destroyed the shrubs and flowers that were their natural habitat. The houses, lawns, and pavements that were created for an expanding human population had, at the same time, evicted at least one species of natural creatures from their own homes. And because one precious living thing had been lost in that community, not only was the harmonious existence of the monarch butterfly disrupted, but also the harmony of Pacific Grove.

Just as you may not pay too much attention to the natural rhythms of nature, so too you may not pay much heed to development, landscaping, harvesting, and other actions that disrupt the harmony that has long been established with your nonhuman, natural "neighbors." When you lose this vision of oneness and begin to see the world as a collection of disparate parts — of islands that supposedly have no impact on surrounding islands — then you lose your ability to live in harmony with nature.

You need to return to a vision of existence that recognizes the part you play in the larger pattern. You're a link in the great chain of being that connects you to and with all of life. And, because of this, you're responsible for maintaining and safeguarding the harmonious connection you have with nature. As writer Henry James once observed, "The touching appeal of nature, as I have called it therefore, the 'Do something kind for me,' is not so much a 'Live upon me and thrive by me' as 'Live *with* me, somehow, and let us make together what we may do for each other — something that is not merely estimable in greasy greenbacks.'"

It's up to you to protect the harmony of your world. So take time to walk around and observe your own neighborhood. Talk to longtime residents about changes that have occurred in the area in the past fifty years. Find out what birds, animals, plants, wildflowers, and trees are in your neighborhood. Develop a deeper understanding of your habitat and learn about any threats to the harmony of your environment. With such awareness comes the possibility for solutions that safeguard the harmony of the many other lives — both human and natural — that share your world.

Protection

*"Teach your children
what we have taught our children —
that the earth is our mother.
Whatever befalls the earth
befalls the sons and daughters of the earth."*

— Suquamish leader Chief Seattle

n 1854 Chief Seattle delivered a speech to the newly arrived Commissioner of Indian Affairs for the Washington Territory. "The Great Chief in Washington sends words that he wishes to buy our land," he began; "...we will consider your offer. For we know that if we do not sell, the white man may come with guns and take our land." Chief Seattle spoke eloquently and emotionally about what the land meant to "the red man," its sacredness to his people. He then said, "The Great Chief sends word he will reserve us a place so that we can live comfortably to ourselves. He will be our father, and we will be his children. So we will consider your offer to buy our land.

But it will not be easy. For this land is sacred to us. This shining water that moves in the streams and rivers is not just water but the blood of our ancestors. If we sell you land, you must remember that it is sacred and that each ghostly reflection in the clear water of the lakes tells of events and memories in the life of the people. The water's murmur is the voice of my father's father....If we sell you our land, you must remember, and teach your children, that the rivers are our brothers and yours, and you must henceforth give the rivers the kindness you would give any brother."

History has recorded Chief Seattle's words; as well, history has recorded how the white man fell short in living up to the Chief's trusting words, words that were based on the promise of protection not only to a nation of people, but also to the nature that the people considered sacred.

Nature teaches you that unless and until humanity can protect every living thing, nature can't protect you. The poisons that are spewed out into the atmosphere poison the very air that you breathe. The fertilizers and pesticides that are sprayed over fields and forests seep into the ground and pollute rivers, streams, and lakes, forcing you to drink bottled water. Fish fill with mercury. Your skin burns quickly and the rate of skin cancer soars because of the depletion of the ozone layer. Gulls and aquatic animals choke on refuse and leaking fuel. Acid rain burns the once-rich soil. Diverted water sources parch water-dependent living things and create deserts out of forests. Prey is eliminated or relocated, causing predator starvation and senseless slaughter. Moose and bear stroll down thoroughfares; hawks roost on the sills of city buildings.

When such things happen, it may seem as if nature has gone crazy, but it's only because of what man has done. As John Rodman, American political scientist has observed, "Not only the beast but the very elements of Nature seem to rise in revolt against man's dominion. The earth, water, and air become noxious with poisons. Man poisons Nature; Nature poisons man in return: the universal Golden Rule.

If you desire to live by the Golden Rule — to do unto others as you wish them to do unto you — then you must offer protection in order to attain it. Henry David Thoreau once wrote that a sparrow alighted on his shoulder for a moment while he was hoeing in a village garden; you could similarly tame a wild animal by consistently showing it no harm. Treating the land and every living creature as if they were your children offers them ultimate protection; what the land and every living creature then returns to you protects the quality of your life. As Chief Seattle has said, "The perfumed flowers are our sisters; the deer, the horse, the great eagle — these are our brothers. The rocky crests, the juices of the meadows, the body heat of the pony, and man — all belong to the same family."

Chief Seattle and his people protected their beloved land by cherishing and respecting it. Will your appetite for living devour the earth and cause it to rebell against you, or will you savor life in ways that protect and preserve it?

Intensity

"Thunder is the voice of God, and, therefore, to be dreaded."

— American clergyman, writer, and college president Increase Mather

When Dorothy, the Tin Man, the Scarecrow, the Lion — and, of course, Toto, too — journeyed to the Emerald City to be granted an audience with The Great and Powerful Oz, they trembled and cowered before the frightening image of Oz that was projected in front of them, startled by the smoke, fire, and thunderous noises that accompanied his commanding voice. But when Toto eventually pulled back the curtain to reveal the true nature of Oz — who was, in reality, a bumbling mortal who needed to manipulate levers and buttons in order to create an image of omnipotence — a more powerful message had been delivered. For what Dorothy and her companions most feared was not the actual image or even the presentation of the image of an all-powerful being that had control over them, but the uncertainty that accompanied the image. What they feared the most was the perception that something bigger than them could — and would — harm or hurt them.

More often than not, nature is gentle with mankind. Winds breathe rhythmically through the trees, rain sprinkles down upon the earth, sunshine warms from a cloudless sky, brooks trickle down hillsides, fog — as American poet Carl Sandburg once so aptly described it — "comes on little cat feet," snow floats down from the sky, frost slowly crystallizes.

But nature also has incredible power

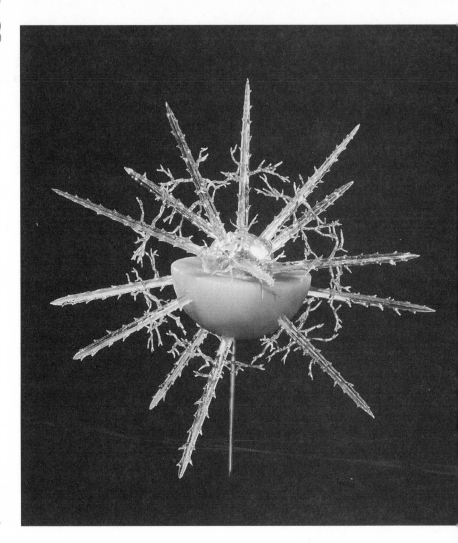

— power that can and does harm and hurt. Volcanoes erupt; fiery lava cascades upon villages and people. Earthquakes split the earth and collapse building floors and highway overpasses, stacking them on top of one another like pancakes. Lightning strikes a powerful match to a dry forest and sends deadly currents into unlucky souls. Tornadoes twist like maniacal screws, boring unpredictable paths that leave death and destruction in their wake. Nor'easters dump tons of snow in blinding winds along coastlines, causing evacuation as well as erosion. Torrential rains flood people out of their cars and homes as well as loosen mudslides that rearrange hillside topography.

No doubt about it — nature can be intense. Because of this, as American humorist Will Rogers once opined, "It's the elements that make you great, or break you." Countless others have discovered how prophetic these words are. In 1982 skilled mountain climber Hugh Herr and his partner Jeffrey Batzer reached the top of Odell's Gully on Mount Washington and decided to push for the summit. They immediately stumbled into a blinding blizzard. Herr and Batzer survived three nights in gale-force winds and below-freezing temperatures. Although they came out alive, Batzer ended up losing one leg; Herr lost both.

But rather than be defeated by his experience, Herr refused to accept any limitations. He designed artificial limbs that enabled him to continue climbing. He invented a more comfortable socket for leg prostheses. He became an advocate of technical solutions to physical disabilities and dreamed of designing artificial legs that would enable those who are physically challenged to run marathons.

To be able to recognize and respect nature's intensity and then to become intense yourself — to courageously face the challenges nature provides — can shift your life from one of complacency and comfort to one that's a daring adventure filled with challenge and change. When you can love nature with such an intense passion that your fear of its incredible power and your joy at its incredible beauty are united, then you're truly living, truly alive.

Whether you seek to scale a mountain peak few have scaled before or decide to conquer a lifelong fear by learning how to swim, what's most important is that you begin to form a relationship with nature's intensity. Strive for something that you think may be beyond your grasp, and what you may find, after striving, is that it really wasn't beyond your grasp at all.

Simplicity

"You already possess everything
necessary to become great."

— Crow proverb

Nothing in nature collects things as obsessively as man does. Garages, kitchen cabinets, linen closets, bookcases, basements, dresser drawers, china closets, table tops, and counters may be filled with items that have been stacked and stockpiled, set aside or cast aside, broken or intact, sometimes dusty with age or lack of use. While a squirrel may collect nuts, a bee pollen, a bird twigs, and a spider insects, such creatures don't seek out those things because they want them but because they need them. That's because all things in nature exist at the "need-level" — seeking only to satisfy needs that are directly related to their survival, such as hunger, thirst, having shelter, and so

on, while man exists at both the need-level as well as the "want-level," going well beyond seeking those things that will ensure survival to reaching a state of mad desire in which the accumulation of possessions, gizmos, gadgets, power, money, and people, as well as consuming in excess, are the goals. Rather than be satisfied with the simple things in life — health, companionship, stability, beauty, wisdom, and comfort — living at such a want-level means you let yourself be assaulted by ceaseless appeals to satisfy insatiable appetites and then readily give in to constant cravings. The more you allow yourself to be assaulted, the more out of control your life can become; soon it's filled with so much clutter and chaos, confusion, and crisis that you have no stability or balance in your life.

In the 1950s a woman who called herself Peace Pilgrim began a walk across America to promote her vision of peace. She set off on her journey only after she had pared down her possessions to what she felt were the essentials — the clothes she was wearing on her back and a few items in her pockets. Living at such a need-level, she rejoiced in the resulting freedom, which she felt both liberated and empowered her. When she was asked why she chose to live so simply, she replied, "A persistent simplication will create an inner and outer well-being that places harmony in one's life."

There are many advantages to living a simpler life, one that's more natural, more need-level. Simplicity clears your vision and allows you to see what you really need as well as what really qualifies as enough. Simplicity frees you from false values, values that rank possessions and endless striving above all else. Simplicity releases old possessions so you can free yourself from the past and live more fully in the present. Simplicity reduces the daily clutter and confusion and restores order in your life. Simplicity shifts the search for security from outside yourself — from things that can become an emotional crutch that provide an illusion of security — to within yourself, to your own innate sense of peace and harmony. Simplicity restores your wholeness, improves your mental health, reduces tension, saves money, decreases pollution, increases a community spirit through sharing, brings greater beauty into your life, and moves you closer to nature.

From this moment on, resolve to live your life more simply. Discard those things you no longer use by recycling what you can and donating other items to charities. Seek out periods of silence each day, times in which you shut out the sensory overload that often assails you from radios, television, the telephone, and mindless chatter. Spend some time each day alone thinking, reading, exercising, or writing in a journal. Meditate on a regular basis. Use your time wisely so you can live a more balanced life. Create daily patterns of stability by choosing a morning ritual of renewal for beginning each day and an evening ritual of closure for ending the day. Enjoy the natural world — take a walk in a park, work in your garden, listen to the songs of birds, smell the flowers, seek out the colors of growing things. Accept the greater peace and joy that you can experience from seeking simplicity.

Timing

"Our lives…have their cycles. Some people are early bloomers, at their peak in high school and their early twenties. Springing up like corn stalks in the hot summer days, they come to harvest in one short season…. While a corn stalk comes to harvest in one short season, an oak tree takes years to mature. But then it towers above the cornfield, its branches reaching toward the sky, bearing fruit for many a season."

— spiritual counselor and writer Diane Dreher

Like everyone else, you go through physical, emotional, and spiritual cycles in your growth. Each time period of your life teaches its own lesson as well as imparts its own gift of change for you. When you were a child, for example, you learned about your world and the people in it, took your first steps, spoke your first words, and began to explore your physical and intellectual capabilities. When you moved out of childhood and into adolescence, your focus shifted to who you were as a person and how you could express this personality to others by developing trust and intimacy. As you grew out of adolescence and into adulthood, you learned lessons in decision-making and responsibility, explored lifestyle choices, and formed moral and spiritual values.

But as you moved out of youth and into maturity, you may have found that your physical, emotional, and spiritual growth experienced cycles of decline and renewal. You may have wandered aimlessly, trying figure out what you wanted to do with your life, while all around you others were forging clear and decisive paths. You may have moved from job to job, location to location, or relationship to relationship to find the best career, the best living situation, and the best partner, while all around you others were landing great jobs, moving into wonderful homes, and dating "Mr./Ms. Right." And you may have felt disheartened because all around you, corn stalks were already shooting up and towering over you — and you had yet to sprout.

Right now you may even be experiencing a period in your life in which you feel joyless, stagnant, bored, listless, and disappointed at how things have turned out for you. You may long to return to early adulthood years that were filled with significant, exciting changes and surges of high energy, similar to the gleeful exultation experienced in spring: "Along the river, over the hills, in the ground, in the sky, spring work is going on with joyful enthusiasm, new life, new beauty, unfolding, unrolling in glorious exuberant extravagance — new birds in their nests, new winged creatures in the air, and new leaves, new flowers, spreading, shining, rejoicing everywhere."

Naturalist John Muir's description of the new life exhibited during one of the eternal cycles of nature — spring's renewal — symbolizes the importance of timing and how nature teaches you to honor timing in your own life. For spring's exuberant renewal is, in reality, simply part of the natural cyclical pattern that eventually transitions to ripening, natural decay, death, and dormancy — and which will transition all over again to renewal. And the process will go on and on.

Like the seasons, you too undergo cycles. Your rhythms replicate the rhythms of nature, cyclical alternations of action and repose, winter and spring, death and rebirth. Understanding such cycles of nature can help you to better understand nature.

Observe nature and learn more about its cycles; what you'll discover is that even though the cycles are relatively predictable, nature is always in flux, always in motion, always changing. Nature never stands still. And so it is with you, too. Observe your own cycles, and you'll find that you never stand still. You're constantly moving, constantly changing, constantly growing. Each day cycles of energy flow within you and around you, giving life to your creation, sustaining it, inspiring it, and taking it through dynamic patterns that help you to know yourself better.

English novelist Charles Dickens once observed, "Nature gives to every time and season some beauties of its own; and from morning to night, as from the cradle to the grave, is but a succession of changes so gentle and easy that we can scarcely mark their progress." The journey of nature, as well as your journey through life, is governed by timing; thus, your ability to pay attention to the impact such timing can make on your life is critical.

Competition

"Then I heard the now familiar honking of the geese flying over the summit ridge at more than 25,000 feet. Heading straight towards their goal, most of them would cross the high peaks in a few days, though some of the weaker birds might not survive the rigors of the journey. Again I wondered why they chose this route. . . .The geese circled the summit once before resuming their flight south. Were they wheeling among the high peaks for the view? For the glory? I smiled and thought, 'I bet they're doing it for the fun of it.'"

— mountaineer Arlene Blum

Have you ever tried to outsmart a squirrel from stealing food from your bird feeders? As your wallet shrinks with the purchase new and improved baffles, repellents, and "squirrel-proof" feeders and as your blood pressure rises at the sight of the squirrel's latest successful assault on your feeder, you may feel as if you're in a head-to-head competition with the furry rodent. The more the squirrel thwarts your efforts, the higher you may feel the competitive stakes go up. Suddenly deterring the squirrel is no longer your goal — it's bringing this "opponent" to its knees so it can emit the defeated cry of, "Nuts!"

Imagine what it would be like if the animal kingdom was as competitive as man. Birds would peck at one another as they strove to build the most striking nest — one that would be featured on the cover of the next issue of *Nest Beautiful*. Hyenas would be giving each other "high-fives" every time they killed a gazelle. Mosquitoes would be excitedly buzzing each morning about their blood-sucking adventures of the previous night. Bees would be awarded blue ribbons for their honey. Peacocks would stage beauty contests. Cheetahs would run 10Ks. Lions would have men's heads stuffed and mounted on the walls of their dens.

Certainly animals compete over many things — territory, nests, mates, and food. Certainly many of the strongest animals survive and many of the weaker ones don't. But although animals must compete with one another — and, oftentimes, with man — for their survival, animals don't think in terms of "us versus them." They don't equate their gains with success and their loses with failure. They don't feel ecstacy with victory or agony with defeat. They set no goals. They live each day without the need to win or lose.

Competition in the animal kingdom is not about glory and gloating, but about the process of living each day. Even if animals could understand, the human concept of competition would be completely incomprehensible to them. As essayist E. B. White has wryly commented, "No two turtles ever lunched together with the idea of promoting anything....Turtles do not work day and night to perfect explosive devices that wipe out Pacific islands and eventually render turtles sterile. Turtles never use the word 'implementation' or the phrases 'hard core' and 'in the last analysis.' No turtle ever rang another turtle back on the phone. In the last analysis, a turtle, although lacking know-how, knows how to live."

In the Orient there are only two ranks in karate — student and master; and only two colors of belt — white and black. But in America karate belts come in a variety of colors: yellow, green, blue, purple, red, and brown. American karate, as well as human nature, is based upon competition — who is measured better, or higher up on the ladder, than another. But Oriental karate instruction, as well as in the animal kingdom, is based upon an individual's progress, regardless of the progress of other students in the class.

Imagine what your life would be like today if society could function more as the animal kingdom does, where there are no corporate ladders, no evidences of low self-esteem and insecurity, no emotions such as envy, no need to tally points. To be able to live in this way, without the need to finish ahead of others and by being content simply to measure your own progress, to go at your own pace, to set your own goals — or to choose not to set any goals at all — allows you to experience more pleasure from life and to do what you'd like to do, simply "for the fun of it."

Death

"If you stand in a meadow, at the edge of a hillside, and look around carefully, almost everything you can catch sight of is in the process of dying, and most things will be dead long before you are. If it were not for the constant renewal and replacement going on before your eyes, the whole place would turn to stone and sand under your feet."

— American physician and writer Lewis Thomas

When scientists studied the lynx in the arctic Hudson Bay region of Canada, they discovered fluctuations in the population that occurred in ten-year cycles. What they also discovered was that the lynx's ten-year cycles coincided with the population changes of the snowshoe hare, its principal prey. At first, researchers attributed the cause of the lynx and hare population cycles to predation, or the regulation of one species of animals by another. Thus, because an increase in the hare population made more food available for the lynx, the number of lynx increased; when the greater number of lynx exerted a higher predation pressure on the hare population, the hare became scarcer; with fewer hare available,

the lynx had difficulty finding prey and became malnourished or diseased and died; with fewer lynx, the hare began to reproduce more offspring, increasing their population; thus, the cycle began again.

But then scientists discovered that while lynx population peaks occasionally coincided with the hare population peaks, sometimes they preceded them rather than followed them, suggesting that predation might not be the only answer. To further complicate their studies, they discovered that on some islands where lynx were absent, the hare populations fluctuated just as much as on the mainland. And when one scientist reported that the reproductive potential of the

hares was so much greater than that of the lynx that the lynx population couldn't possibly exterminate the hare population to match the numbers that had been shown, another explanation had to be discovered.

What had happened? After some study it was determined that the hare's habitat, rather than predation by the lynx, controlled the size of the hare's population. When the hare population increased, their food supply was more rapidly depleted, which led to their own decline. So the hare population, rather than another species, regulated itself without impacting on another species or further depleting its own food supply so it could ensure the survival of future generations of hare and of species that needed the hare for their own survival.

However, such essential regulation doesn't take place in society. For example, whenever a city's population increases, water departments simply drill more wells, which drain the local aquifers to dangerous levels, or import water from distant lakes and rivers, which severely impacts natural habitats. Rather than set population limits in certain areas by restricting development, mankind prefers that rivers and lakes — and the wildlife that depend upon such water sources — are disrupted.

Depletion, whether natural or man-made, causes death. Nature has no way of communicating with humanity that something has become so dangerously depleted that every living thing is in jeopardy; oftentimes mankind discovers too late the folly of ignoring the impact human population can have. Left alone, nature can renew itself without assistance from man. But once man impacts upon nature for his own benefit, nature becomes dependent upon man to restore order.

Nature teaches you, through the laws of predation as well as through natural limits to growth, that the concept of carrying capacity is key. The question you always need to be unafraid to ask is, "How many people in this area where I live can be adequately supported in a healthy condition over a relatively long period of time without doing damage to the environment?"

In nature, long before any real damage can be done by any majority population, environmental limits kick in to protect and preserve. In society, it's up to you — and to every individual — to help set such limits. As American conservationist and writer Aldo Leopold warns, "Wilderness is a resource which can shrink but not grow…the creation of a new wilderness in the full sense of the word is impossible."

Birth

*"This I understand: Mother Nature is a maniac.
That is to say, she has a mania for reproduction. She maintains
life within an organism so long as there is hope of its reproducing
itself. Then she kills it off, and does so in the most diverse ways
because of her other mania of remaining mysterious."*

— Italian writer Italo Svevo

Sometimes your life may seem to be the same old story, repeated over and over again each day, each week, each month, each year. Aside from a brief vacation, holiday, or day trip that may interrupt your story, you may feel that your life is pretty much predictable and, because of this, awfully dull and uninteresting. You may get up each morning and follow the same morning routine. Then you may go off to work or school or begin household tasks. You may come in contact with the same people. You may eat lunch at about the same time, sometimes eating the same packed lunch or ordering the same sandwich day after day. You may eat dinner at about the same time each evening

and engage in the same evening routine — watching television, battling with your children over homework assignments, sorting through your mail, and so on. Your weekends may revolve around running errands or catching up with all the things you didn't get to during the week or spending time with all the people you didn't get to see. After awhile you may find your story so repetitiously mind-numbing that you moan, "What kind of life is this? There's no life in my life!"

Yet all of life is filled with such predictable and eternal cycles. In nature, night always turns into day. Winter always turns into spring. Tides always go in and out. Leaves always turn colors in autumn. When you think about it, every day, every week, every month, every year in nature repeats the same old story. As American humorist Dorothy Parker once joked, "Every year, back spring comes, with the nasty little birds yapping their fool heads off, and the ground all mucked up with arbutus. Year after year after year."

But nature is able to transform the seemingly tired old story it offers the world into a charming, interesting book filled with wonderous chapters. It does this by constantly renewing itself with vigor and fresh life. In the spring this is most evident, with robins returning from their winter homes and chirruping from sun-up to sun-down; with the popping and cracking sound of ice melting on rivers and the gurgling of cold streams rushing down mountainsides; with the green blades of flowers and grasses heaving clumps of earth out of their way. Summer yields a steady and energetic growth, and autumn reveals a freshness in crisp brilliance that belies the oncoming stillness of winter.

Yet even in winter there's new growth; prolonged periods of cold temperatures and dormancy are necessary for trees to blossom and bear fruit, for roots to push deep into the ground to support lush new green life, and for animals to conserve their energy in order to mate and give birth. The endless cycles of nature create thousands of living things year after year, gradually bring them into decline, then create new life. On and on and on the same story goes — a story that has remained unchanged for centuries.

But what may make nature's story far more interesting than yours is nature's ability to transform itself from year to year — to give birth to millions of new, living things, each with something unique and special to contribute to the normal flow of everyday life. "There's the first robin!" you may cry out each spring with much excitement and enthusiasm. Why do you delight over such a predictable sight? And why can't you bring the same level of excitement about the return of the same species of bird at about the same time each year — year after year after year — into your own life?

You, too, are being reborn every minute of the day; every cell in your body is constantly changing. You're not the same person you were even just a few minutes ago. So you can, if you want, transform the eternal cycles in your life. Look for the larger patterns in your life — the impact your work makes, for instance, rather than the daily tasks you perform or what physical shape you'd be in if you didn't exercise every day. Look, inside yourself. As Henry David Thoreau once recommended, "We must learn to reawaken and keep ourselves awake.... Every man is tasked to make his life, even in its details, worthy of the contemplation of his most elevated and critical hour."

Remember that you get what you cultivate in your life. Think of yourself and your life as a garden, and then keep in mind what will happen if you don't plant new seeds each year, tend to them, and cultivate their growth. So if you focus solely on how dull and lifeless the story of your daily life is, then you'll feel dull and lifeless; your garden will become choked with weeds and nothing will reach fruition. But if, instead, you focus on living wholeheartedly — let your roots go deep into everything you do so you become immersed into the people, places, and things in your life — then you can transcend the monotony of your eternal cycles and transform them into freshness, gladness, and ecstacy. You can give birth to a whole new story, filled with charming chapters, sweet inscriptions, and exciting vignettes.

Change

" 'I shouldn't be surprised if it hailed a good deal tomorrow,'
Eeyore was saying. 'Blizzards and whatnot. Being fine today doesn't
Mean Anything. It has no sig — what's that word? Well, it has
none of that. It's just a small piece of weather.' "

— English poet and writer A.A. Milne

Try predicting the weather. One way to do so is by studying the clouds, to learn how to read changing cloud patterns through the recognition of common cloud shapes and what they mean. Look up in the sky during the day; the height of the clouds is one signal of approaching weather. For example, you can expect a storm if high, scattered puffy cumulus clouds or horizontally flattened stratus clouds get thicker, increase in number, or get low and dark in the sky. If the sky's webbed with high, icy wisps of clouds — cirrus clouds — that may be a signal that warmer, wetter weather is on the way. If low, dense clouds rise higher and decrease in number, this can mean fair weather is sure to arrive. Or, if you look up in the sky during the night, a halo-like ring around the moon may mean approaching precipitation.

As well, you can pay attention to the way in which the wind is blowing; storms typically blow in from the west, moving from Chicago to New England in about a day's time. You can try to predict the weather from old rhymes or beliefs, such as "Red sky at morning, sailors take warning; Red sky at night, sailors' delight," or "Big snowflakes, little snowfall; little snowflakes, big snowfall." You can observe how vigorously squirrels collect nuts in order to determine how harsh an upcoming winter may be. You can pay attention to whether the ground hog sees its shadow as an indication of how much longer winter will last.

But no matter how closely you observe the most important signals for approaching weather — or even if you studied meteorology yourself — what you'll soon discover is that the most predictable thing about the menu of the day that nature has to offer is its unpredictability. Forecasters warn of heavy snowfalls that turn into dustings or predict a cool, cloudy day that turns out to be a picture-perfect beach day — hot, sunny, and without a cloud in the sky. Tornadoes suddenly whirl into existence, earthquakes shake foundations and split the earth without warning, and gale winds get stirred up for no apparent reason. About the most reliable forecast that has ever been given was once offered by comedian George Carlin, who said, "Weather forecast for tonight: dark."

Amidst the eternal cycles of nature are the unpredictable, surprising moments that catch you completely off-guard — without an umbrella or raincoat, without an ice scraper, without gloves, without a windbreaker, without a hat. There's little you can

do when this happens but simply get through it; you know, however, that whatever small pieces of weather that happen are temporary.

So, too, it is with many of the small pieces of weather that happen in your life — the unexpected things for which you're not prepared. This includes the things that don't always go as planned, such as a well-thought-out dinner party, or accidental occurrences, such as a chance meeting that results in a long-term relationship. From such things you know that life can be quite unpredictable. Sometimes the unpredictability catches you off-guard and changes your life in marvelous ways; sometimes the unpredictability throws you an incredible challenge; sometimes the unpredictability forces you to give up something or someone you cherished.

Changes abound in life; without change, life wouldn't be an ongoing process of birth, death, and renewal. Change keeps you from staying in dead-end jobs and unhappy relationships. Change helps you to improve hopeless situations. Change encourages you to trust the unknown. Change conquers fear and develops courage. Change releases your need to control everything and everybody. Change urges you to take positive action. Change supports you in doing your best. Change teaches you about limitations and how to challenge them. Change helps you to come face to face with yourself. Change alters your vision of life. As an unknown soul once observed, "There is more to be learned on one day of discomfort, poverty, and anxiety than in a lifetime of apparent happiness, security, riches, and power."

So rather than yearn to live in a predictable, yet boring climate, where everything always stays the same, relish the experience of change that nature — and life — provides for you through the small pieces of weather that come your way each day.

Faith

"This grand show is eternal. It is always sunrise somewhere; the dew is never all dried at once; a shower is forever falling; vapor is ever rising. Eternal sunrise, eternal sunset, eternal dawn and gloaming, on sea and continents and islands, each in its turn, as the round earth rolls."

— American naturalist John Muir

Some people, when faced with a loss, conflict, problem, or other difficulty, can only feel sorrow, worry, tension, and stress. Back and forth their emotions go as they alternate between crying and trembling. "What am I going to do now?" they may nervously question as they wring their hands. "Where will I go? What shall I do? How am I going to get through this time? Is it always going to be this way?" Such fear-filled thoughts imprison them, paralyze them, dishearten them, sicken them, and detract them from taking the steps necessary to get through their tough time.

It has been said that the opposite of such fearfulness is faith. But how can you change your fears into faith when times

are tough — when pain, illness, sadness, depression, grief, separation, or other difficulties sometimes feel so overpowering and all-encompassing that they seem to take on a life of their own? For that matter, if you have little or no faith to begin with, how do you start having faith?

An old story once told by Chuang Tzu describes a man who was so afraid of his own shadow and the sound of his footsteps that he ran away from them. But the more he ran, the louder the footsteps sounded and the more swiftly his shadow raced after him. The man's fears soon grew into panic, and he ran faster and faster until he finally died of exhaustion. What the man didn't realize is that if he had only stopped running and rested under the shade of a tree, the shadow would have disappeared and the footsteps would have ceased.

Nature can dispel many of the shadows in life that cause you fear. Look outside your window on a winter day and remember that the trees, now bare, will soon bud. The ground, now frozen and snow-covered, will soon thaw. The bulbs you planted last fall, now dormant, will soon break through the ground and blossom. The robins will soon return from their winter vacation, along with the summer songbirds. Rain will sometimes fall, winds will blow, thunder will rumble and roar, and lightning will flash, but the skies will also clear so that the sun can shine brightly through. The strong limbs of the trees will branch out and sprout broad green leaves that will provide shelter from the heat.

If you have faith that the spring renewal will always arrive and that the winter winds will always eventually die out, then you can also have faith that you'll get through any time of crisis. For, as writer Robert L. Veninga once penned, "It is true that as we take two steps forward in our journey, we may take one or more steps backward. But when one has faith that the spring thaw will arrive, the winter winds seem to lose some of their punch."

There's a season to every crisis; each crisis goes through a natural cycle of birth, life, and death, just as everything else in nature does. Trusting this means having faith in things; once you have faith in things, you can have faith in people; once you have faith in things and people, you can have faith in yourself — and then there's no stopping the strengthening and growth of your faith.

One of the most basic laws of nature is that nature heals with faith. Nature teaches you that nothing — ever — lasts forever and that nothing — ever — continues with the same intensity with which it began. Accept this law, and you'll have the courage to seek solutions to all of your difficulties rather than be ruled by fear. Trust this law, and you'll be able to trust that you can get through any hard time, no matter how hard it may seem at any given moment. With such courage and trust, you will then have the faith to say, with confidence and assurance, "I will get through this tough time." There can be no fear where there is such faith.

Spiritualist leader Rabindranath Tagore once offered that, "Faith is the bird that feels the light and sings when the dawn is still dark." The bird trusts that the sky will soon lighten, the sun will rise, and the world will come alive.

16 Patience

*"The wildcat does not make enemies
by rash action. He is observant, quiet, and tactful,
and he always gains his ends."*

— Pawnee proverb

In 1983 zoologist Alan Rabinowitz ventured into the rain forest of Belize, Central America, to study the jaguar in its natural habitat and to establish the world's first jaguar preserve. As he began his research, he discovered that the hours flew by, but he had few results to show for the amount of time he had spent hard at work. He was also dismayed at the pace at which the villagers worked — much slower than his own — and at the fact that equipment often took months to arrive or to be repaired. As time plodded along, Rabinowitz started to lose faith in his mission. "It no big ting man," the villagers would tell him. "Saafly, saafly [softly, softly], tiger ketch monkey" —

meaning that Rabinowitz would get what he wanted, eventually.

It has been said that, "To make a peach you need a winter, a summer, an autumn and a bee, so many nights and days and sun and rain, petals rosy with pollen — all that your mouth may know a few minutes of pleasure." So, too, it is in your life; for anything worthwhile to be accomplished, you need to be patient. If all you have in sight is the end — in reaching a particular goal or completing a particular project — then you may set off blindly on a task before you've had time to think about it, pressure yourself and others around you to pick up the pace, or search for distracting, and sometimes defeating, shortcuts.

Everyone likes to bring a project to completion or reach a longed for goal; no matter what its size or importance, attaining what you desire can bring about feelings of exhileration and a sense of accomplishment. Yet being too obsessed with closure can result in carelessness or the need to stop to make time-consuming repairs. Thus, patience is a necessary ingredient you need to add to all the tasks you're trying to complete.

There's the story of a man who owned a peach orchard who learned a valuable lesson in patience. One year he harvested a crop of much smaller peaches than usual. He apologized to all of his customers, explaining that his orchards needed constant attention. He said that it often took him an entire day to prune one tree properly, and with over five hundred trees to tend, he couldn't keep up with the difficulty and expense of the project. "This makes me very upset," he confided to one of his regular customers. "Why can't I prune all of my trees properly? I tried rushing through the job, but ended up severely damaging some of the trees in my haste. So I decided to let the trees grow as they wanted to. And this is what happened," he sighed as he indicated the smaller peaches with a wave of his hand.

The customer took a bite of a smaller peach, then smiled. "This is the most delicious peach I've ever tasted," she said. "Even though the peaches are smaller, they're even more tasty. Maybe letting the trees grow as they wanted to was a good thing."

Impatience is a quality that's not only alien to nature, but life-threatening. A spider that weaves a web too quickly will be left with unconnected strands. A bird that builds a nest in haste will find itself without a safe place for its eggs. A hawk that swoops too soon at a field mouse will soar back up into the sky empty-handed. A flower that blooms before spring's warmth will die. A lion that jumps too soon at its prey will return to its den hungry.

Nature's living things are inherently patient. Each creature lives by its cycles, in a world with a spare but life-sustaining economy, and does nothing to interfere with the pattern of life that has been created for its benefit. That which comes to it is accepted; that which does not come to it is not its concern. As Ralph Waldo Emerson once advised, "Adopt the pace of nature: her secret is patience." This is a most valuable piece of advice, but are you patient enough to follow it?

Stillness

"One of the best places you can go in a canoe is the wilderness. And what, you may ask, is so great about that? The silence, for one thing. In real wilderness, silence is not just quiet, which is the absence of noise. It is the voice of the living earth, unmuddied by aural clutter."

— naturalist Robert Kimber

Imagine that every time you're assailed by unwanted noise — from planes, trains, automobiles, and tractor-trailer trucks; from jackhammers, chainsaws, motorboats, Jetskis, and snowmobiles; from honking horns, screeching brakes, and angry people; from slamming doors, barking dogs, and radio commercials; and from countless other sources, whether you live in the city or the country — a fine red dust drifts down upon you. The Eastern religion of Taoism uses this symbol of red dust to refer to those things in the world that are hard to brush away and that keep the mind from becoming still. But, as Taoist writer Deng Ming-Dao interprets from the book of *Tao,* "Once the red dust passes,/The mind is still."

The noise of modern life can make it hard for you to participate in conversations so you can listen intently and converse with another in a calm, soothing manner. Radios drone in your car or home, piped-in music follows you from work to the grocery store to the shopping mall, and the television is an ever-present background noise. Turning on the radio or television the minute you get home from work and keeping it on until you go to bed can even make it hard for you to hear yourself think, for how can pay attention to your own thoughts when your mind is being invaded by the concerns of fictional characters who speak their false words between interruptions of blaring consumer messages?

Sometimes it may seem as if there's no escape from any sort of invasive noise. Go to the beach, and rather than hear the gentle cries of the gulls or the soothing sounds of the waves lapping the shore, you're assailed by the screams of unhappy children and the thumping beat of competing radios. Get away from the city noise and rent a cabin by a lake for a week, and rather than be gently awakened by the cries of loons calling out to one another, you may be rattled out of bed by machines that clear the land to build homes and cut down trees or by the incessant whining of motorboats as they race around the lake.

When was the last time you heard the wind as it gently stirred long blades of grass, the sound of a gentle summer rain caressing a lake, or the call of geese flying overhead? Too much red dust coats you and clogs your ears. As long as the aural stimulations of the world continue to swirl around you and blow through your mind, the true stillness of nature will evade you.

Indian spiritual leader Mahatma Gandhi sought out periods of silence by setting aside a day of silence a week. No matter what happened on that day or who came to visit, he would spend the day quietly, communicating to others only in writing. Could you maintain an entire day in such silence? A few hours? A few minutes?

Nature teaches you about silence in the stillness of a forest, a quiet lake, a rugged mountainside, a squirrel foraging for food, a flock of geese floating on a pond, a field of wildflowers, puffy clouds in the sky, the moon illuminating a blanket of snow. But it may not be easy to seek such natural silences without traveling a great distance or rearranging a hectic schedule.

You can, however, seek such stillness from within. Establish a regular time for meditation in which you divorce yourself from the hubbub of the world for at least fifteen minutes and sit quietly by yourself and with yourself. Use slow, conscious breathing to focus your energy, slow your mind down, and help you to "go within" — to places deep beneath the noise and surface clatter. It may help to visualize yourself in a still place in nature, such as on a mountaintop. Or, if you can, you can actually go out into nature and sit on a rock in a nearby woods or on a blanket at the seashore.

Close your eyes and sit quietly, slowly emptying your mind of its clutter. Gradually withdraw from the voices of everyday life; learn to pay heed only the voice of silence. Even short periods of such stillness, practiced on a regular basis, can bring you closer to an understanding of the stillness of nature. As Ralph Waldo Emerson once remarked about naturalist Henry David Thoreau, "Thoreau knew how to sit immovable, a part of the rock he rested on, until the bird, the reptile, the fish, which had retired from him should come back and resume its habits — nay, moved by curiosity, should come back to him and watch him." Seek the silence, still the mind, and you'll soon feel the strength in the silence.

18 Wisdom

Go my sons, burn your books,
Buy yourselves stout shoes.
Get away to the mountains, the deserts
And the deepest recesses of the earth.
In this way and no other will you gain
A true knowledge of things and
Of their properties.

— Seter Severinus (1571 A.D.)

Who is wiser — the person who knows that Shakespeare wrote the play *Romeo and Juliet*, or someone who wonders who wrote the songs the birds sing? The one who knows how to make homemade ice cream, or someone who thinks that ice cream tastes happy? The one who can name all the oceans of the world, or someone who questions whether the sea — and not just all of the creatures in it — is alive? Who is wiser — the person who has knowledge about most things and how they work, or the one who questions everything in the environment, seeking understanding? What, for that matter, is wisdom? Is it the accumulation of more and more information, sort of an encyclopedic knowledge type of feeding frenzy, or the ability to memorize poems, passages from classics or religious texts, and mathematical formulas?

Some people think that those who memorize a great deal and remember much of it are wise. Others — mostly the young, because they have a mania for information in the data-saturated world in which they live — believe that accumulation of facts and figures is evidence of their wisdom. Still others hold that a lifetime filled with adventure is what creates wisdom.

While it's true that a crucial part of life is seeking knowledge, mere accumulation and management of data doesn't necessarily build wisdom. While it's true that adventure can expand one's horizons, sometimes the process of seeking adventure can actually prevent the development of a certain level of maturity that's necessary for wisdom. Living somewhat haphazardly, from adventure to adventure, can sometimes inhibit the ability to be secure in time and place as well as with oneself. And sometimes, in seeking knowledge of the world in which you live, what you may learn may be far from pleasant; in fact, with such learning you may glimpse life as it really is and may find this too difficult to bear without being able to temper what you've learned with an experiential element.

Wisdom is not simply a mental process, but the sum total of a human being. What this means is that if you can mix what you know with what you've learned through your experiences, your adventures, your experimentations, the risks you've taken, your spiritual beliefs, the people you've met, the intimacies you've shared, and the insights you've gained during times of introspection and contemplation, then you can be said to be wise. Wisdom is the bridge that connects the facts you've accumulated with what you can intuit about yourself and life. As well, it's the ability to be able to live somewhat haphazardly from time to time — to accept that life isn't always clear-cut,

that it doesn't always provide you with meaningful patterns or reassuring understandings, but often mixes the good with the bad, the ugly with the beautiful, the successes with the failures, the sweet with the bitter, the mistakes with the victories.

Wisdom is knowing as well as not knowing, and not being bothered by such ambiguity. As writer and amateur stargazer Barry Evans writes, "...it's about awareness: noticing, stopping, looking, heeding, remarking, observing, beholding, discerning, perceiving, asking, examining, probing, considering, pondering, weighing, appraising, studying... right now. It's about wonder....It's about stopping and noticing phenomena in the world around us — air, water, light, gravity, breath, dolphins, rocks, wind, and heartbeats — and appreciating them more for understanding them a little."

To gain wisdom, keep yourself open, receptive, and perceptive. Make yourself a part of every aspect of the world. Be bold. Participate. Use your senses. Tolerate uncertainty, confusion, ignorance, and suspense. Then, with the wisdom you've gained by doing such things, combined with the knowledge you've learned, you'll gradually begin to make some sense out of life.

Nurturing

*"The creator created the Earth, our Mother Earth,
and gave her many duties, among them to care for us, His people.
He put things upon Mother Earth for the benefit of all.
As we travel around today we see that our Mother Earth is still
doing her duty, and that we are very grateful."*

— Onondaga chief Irving Powless, Sr.

Even when ponds begin to ice over with the coming winter, fish can survive in the frigid depths for months. The water nurtures the fish, providing the aquatic life with enough oxygen and food to nurture and sustain life. As you sit by the edge of the frozen pond lacing up your ice skates, you may be totally unaware of how dependent the pond and the fish are upon one another. Without the fish to keep the water free from algae, the pond would eventually become choked with weeds and grow stagnant; without the water, the fish would be helpless. So both the fish and the water nurture one another in a mutually agreeable and beneficial interconnectedness.

The ocean, too, is another nurturing, life-sustaining, interdependent force. The seabirds, fish, coral, the tiny crustaceans, giant whales, and many other creatures depend upon the ocean. The life that lives in and around it is one with the ocean; the ocean is one with all it touches, from the rivers that flow from the mountains into the sea to the people who live on distant shores. The Atlantic Ocean nurtures and sustains life from North America to Europe and Africa; it pools northward to the Arctic Ocean and south through the straits of Magellan to the Pacific Ocean; it flows to the Antarctic Sea and back into itself, providing one enormous nurturing embrace of life to all

the seven continents of the world and the entire Planet Earth.

These are just two examples of why it's so important that you understand the lesson that nature teaches you about nurturing. The world's current ecological problems remind you on a daily basis that you're not a separate entity but a significant part in the complex web of life. Any noncaring action — illegal disposal of a hazardous product, an oil spill, the use of road salt near rivers and lakes, spraying chemicals near a wildlife population's water source, using nets that capture tuna but also kill dolphins, or using chemical fertilizers on land that slowly seep into the water supply and out to sea — can produce immediate harmful reactions that then extend out from the source and far along the chain of life.

Water is one of nature's most valuable, and most nurturing, resources. Each day, you use nearly a thousand gallons of water for personal use at your home and in your place of work. Five to seven gallons of pure water are polluted every time you flush a toilet. Fruit, grain, and vegetable farms; agriculturally based businesses such as the beef and poultry industries; power plants; and manufacturing facilities use incredible amounts of water. Taking for granted that

there will always be an unlimited supply of fresh, clean water every time you turn on the tap is similar to the mentality of those who rode the transcontinental railroad as it sped westward, leaned out of windows, and fired indiscriminantly at the placid buffalo, killing thousands, leaving their bodies to rot in the dust and causing near extinction.

When you not only take nature's nurturing living things for granted but also take from nature in large quantities without thought of replenishing what you've used, then the nurturing relationship you and nature have with one another can't be maintained. For, as Vice President Al Gore once pointed out, "The rains bring us trees and flowers; the droughts bring gaping cracks in the world. The lakes and rivers sustain us; they flow through the veins of the earth and into our own. But we must take care to let them flow back out as pure as they came, not poison and waste them without thought for the future."

Employing personal conservation habits can make a difference. Conserve water by using it more consciously, and become more aware of the quality of water in nearby lakes, streams, rivers, and bays. Be grateful for the nurturing of Mother Earth; show your gratitude by returning such nurturing in kind.

Sex

"To her children nature seems to have said,
'Copulate you must. But beyond that there is no rule.
Do it in whatever way and with whatever emotional
concomitants you choose. That you should do it
somehow or other is all that I ask.'"

— writer Joseph Wood Krutch

Study after study has shown that the male and female strategies for sexual behavior are often worlds apart. For the male, whose initial investment in any sexual liasion is minimal, promiscuity is of utmost importance; his rallying cry, not surprisingly, is "Quantity, not quality!" The female, on the other hand, cares more for the quality of her partner and is very selective, discriminantly choosing only a few good mates from many potential suitors. While the attraction of a potential mate is a top priority for both males and females, to then be able to arouse and sustain sexual interest in one another as well as to synchronize each partner's sexual drive for mutual satisfaction can be hard — if not impossible — to orchestrate, particularly when mates sometimes have conflict of interest.

Even when everything seems to be going well between the male and the female, sometimes the female gets scared and flees from the male in fear. This can be fear over the possibility of sexual involvement as well as fear over the male's overly aggressive, possessive, or even obsessive behavior. Or the female may display ambivalent feelings to the male — showing him a sort of "whatever" type of attitude when he's going to great lengths to impress her — or she may confuse him by sending out

62

mixed messages such as "Come close, go away" or "I'm staying, now I'm leaving." But once the fear is dealt with and the female makes her decision, oftentimes the flames of arousal can be sparked and sex can occur.

Or, then again, maybe it won't. Instead, the male and female may actively court one another for some time. The male may try to dazzle the female by proudly displaying his finery, strength, or capabilities; he may even engage in competitions with other males in order to impress the female. The female, as well, may play her own courtship-like games — sometimes feigning disinterest at the male's efforts to impress her or sometimes sending out distinct signals that are designed to attract, arouse, and convey a readiness for sex.

While this description may sound like human mating behaviors, it's really a description of animal sexual behavior. Even though a male and female may belong to the same species in the animal kingdom and have an equal desire to have sex, that doesn't necessarily mean they'll be sexual partners. As in the human kingdom, there's a bit more selectivity involved; such selectivity can include complicated and lengthy courtship displays and rituals, intense competition between males of the same species over one female, and, in many cases, rejection of potential suitors by disinterested or fearful females. The "sex game" can be just as dicey with animals as it is with humans; not surprisingly, it's often because the genders are at odds with one another. Because the males view sex as a competitive sport and the females focus on whether the male is a good genetic specimen and whether he will help raise the young, the males of many species often participate in interesting rituals designed to attract the females of their species. Arabian oryxes stiffen their forelegs to court their mates. Birds of paradise hang upside down and flaunt their beautiful plummage. Tortoise mates ram shells, trying to flip each other over. A bulk elk bugles during breeding season to advertise his territory and attract females.

But it's not just the animal kingdom that flaunts its sexual behavior. As Diane Ackerman writes, "A flower's fragrance declares to all the world that it is fertile, available, and desirable, its sex organs oozing with nectar. Its smell reminds us in vestigial ways of fertility, vigor, life-force, all the optimism, expectancy, and passionate bloom of youth. We inhale its ardent aroma and, no matter what our age, we feel young and nubile in a world aflame with desire."

There's little difference between nature and humankind when it comes to sexual behavior; members of both species primp and preen, emit enticing aromas to attract potential partners, play coy games with one another, engage in ritualistic courting behaviors, seek a desirable as well as an appealing partner, communicate attraction, and act on their attractions.

Sex is a natural part of living, shared with every living thing. As such, it should always be respected — never used as leverage or manipulation or selfishness or abuse. It should be treated as the most mysterious, sacred, and profound interaction two people can share. Whether what's created is a relationship or a pregnancy, the legacy of both partners will be inherent in their creation.

Beauty

"The path through the woods has a light layer of scarlet leaves that have fallen early from the woodbine. Crickets are chirping the coming of a new season — and the sassy blue jay, tla yu ga, agrees....The pulse of the earth slows our own and tranquilizes confusion. Seeing the ga lv lo i, sky, in its limitless depths stirs us to imagine, to stretch our awareness to know how much beauty is provided for us."

— writer Joyce Sequichie Hifler

Imagine that a visitor from another planet has asked you to show evidences of beauty in order to understand what beauty means to you and other members of Planet Earth. You might decide to take the visitor to some of the country's national parks, pointing out such beautiful things as pine trees and scenic vistas, sparkling clear lakes and gushing waterfalls, the Grand Canyon at sunset, the eruption of Old Faithful. Or you might decide to take the visitor on a walking tour of the beaches of Cape Cod or for a ride along the breathtaking Pacific coastline. You might decide that the visitor will learn a great deal about beauty by camping in the wilderness or hiking to the top of a majestic mountain. Or you might believe that exploring underground caves will capture beauty. After taking the visitor on a whirlwind tour of many locations throughout America, you might then decide to take the visitor to foreign lands.

Imagine that you're on your way to the airport to fly off to yet another destination that will provide further evidence of beauty when the alien suddenly points out the window of the taxicab while you're stuck in traffic. "There's beauty! There's beauty!" the alien shouts. You lean forward and look out the window in the direction the visitor is indicating, but can't see anything but trash and broken glass behind a dented metal road barrier.

"I don't see anything," you reply, shaking your head.

"There! There!" the visitor says excitedly. "The color! The yellow! Oh, what do you call it? See there? The thing that smells!"

You squint your eyes and suddenly see a tiny bunch of buttercups swaying in the exhaust-heavy breeze.

"There is beauty, yes?" the visitor asks. "For it is not where it ought to be, out in those great, wide, open spaces far away from your home — those places you've gone to great time and expense to show me. But here it is right near you, for you to see every time you drive by. See? Now you don't have to go so far away. You can just come here any time and see such beauty that is living right with you."

You may feel that you live in a day-to-day world that feels too ugly, too violent, too disgusting, too filthy, too vulgar, and too brutal to support natural beauty. Because of this, you may think that the only natural beauty that could possibly exist in the world is in "the great outdoors" — far away from your back door, apartment balcony, or work location.

And yet the beauty of nature exists right alongside you. Wildflowers grow along littered highways. Trees line city streets filled with run-down triple deckers. Squirrels scamper and play near park benches occupied by the sick, drunk, and homeless. Hawks roost and raise families on massive bridges where the hopeless end their lives. On gritty city sidewalks, in the shadows of massive buildings, vendors display cheap plastic buckets filled with fragrant fresh flowers.

It has been said that even on the road to hell, flowers grow. Although fragile and easily destroyed, they can also be hardy and persistent. Pull one out, and another will grow in its place. Pave the earth, and they'll find a way to poke through a tiny crack. They're delicate, but determined. Plant them in a garden, tend to them, and watch them grow, and you're rewarded for your efforts by their beautiful display. But come across them unexpectedly, out of their element and in a constant struggle against the elements, and you're truly blessed.

Writer George Orwell once said, "Indeed it is remarkable how Nature goes on existing unofficially, as it were, in the very heart of London." Appreciate nature's "unofficial" existence whereever you go as a blessing that's been bestowed upon you. Then you can truly know what beauty is.

Perfection

*"Use what talents you have;
the woods would have little music if no birds sang
their song except those who sang best."*

— Reverend Oliver G. Wilson

One day, a Vietnam veteran who was recovering from the loss of his legs asked one of his physical therapists, "What good is all this rehabilitation doing? I'm never going to be as good as other men who have two legs. I'm still going to leave this hospital a hopeless cripple."

The therapist replied, "It's true that you'll leave here a helpless cripple as long as you focus on only one thing — what you've lost. But what about all those things you still have; a strong body, a fully functioning mind, and the potential of things to come? Just because someone else may have two arms, two legs, and all their senses intact doesn't mean they aren't handicapped in other ways —

emotionally, creatively, motivationally, or spiritually — in ways that you aren't." Today this veteran works with paraplegics, challenging them in the same way his physical therapist challenged him.

Everyone and everything in nature has limitations and imperfections. Just as there's no such thing as a perfect person, neither is there such a thing as a perfect living thing. There are certainly quite attractive people, there are certainly creative people, and there are certainly charismatic people, but there are no perfect people. Too, in nature there are wonderfully fragrant roses, there are roses with soft, velvety petals, and there are symmetrically shaped roses, but there are no perfect roses.

Yet at those times when you're feeling down or when you lose confidence in yourself for whatever reason, it may be easy to doubt not only your perfection, but also that you're even good at anything. When such self-doubt and low confidence sets in, it may be tempting to compare yourself to others — to those whom you aspire to emulate because you think that who they are and what they do qualifies them as being the best. As you look over photographs you've taken, for example, you may think, "I'm no Ansel Adams." As you reread a poem you've written, you may decide, "I'm no Emily Dickinson." As you assess your current position in business, you may conclude, "I'm no Bill Gates." Or you may tell the parent in you, "You're no Dr. Spock."

Such critical messages have an uncanny way of making you feel inferior even before you attempt to do something. They can also hurt or damage your attitude about your creativity and talents so you give up even trying. "After all," you might think, "I'll never be *that* good!"

But can you imagine any living thing in nature engaging in such comparisons or feeling a similar sense of inferiority? One daisy doesn't look about the field of daisies it's in and think, "Geez, I'm just not as pretty as the others." One red ant doesn't look at another red ant and think, "Wow! Look at that big crumb he's hauling! I'll never be as strong as that!" One bird doesn't perch on a limb of a tree, listening to the melodious song of another, and then sigh, "I might as well give up singing — my song won't ever measure up to that one!"

Nature teaches you that every living thing is valuable and has its important place and vital contribution to make. As Ralph Waldo Emerson once commented, "What is a weed? A plant whose virtues have not yet been discovered." Each rose, each daisy, each ant, each songbird — even each weed — manifests its potential differently, yet beautifully. Each living thing in nature has its own expression, its own fragrance, its own capabilities, its own skills, its own song. Only human beings suffer from a low sense of self-esteem.

There will always be people in the world who are better than you in some way. Rather than bemoan this fact or let it get you down, accept yourself as you are. Focus on what you possess and know that you, too, are great simply because you're another living thing — another miracle of nature.

23 Suffering

*"You will forget your misery;
you will remember it as waters
that have passed away."*

— Job 11:16

You know that all wounds need time to heal, whether the wounds be physical, emotional, or spiritual. But when you've been wounded — by an illness or injury, by the loss of a relationship or loved one, or by a sense of hopelessness and despair — you may believe that you'll never be able to heal. You may feel that from that moment on, you'll always be in pain or you'll always feel sad, empty, hopeless, depressed, lost, and lonely. Suffering will become your permanent state of living; your suffering will have no end.

Yet no present hour ever endures; nothing in the universe stands still. The saying "And this, too, shall pass away" provides an apt reminder that the world's a scene of perpetual change, constant in its inconstancy. As D. H. Lawrence wrote, "Where are the little yellow aconites of eight weeks ago? I neither know nor care. They were sunny and the sun shines, and sunniness means change, and petals passing and coming."

Rather than sit around and bemoan your suffering, use this difficult time to work with the natural cycles of change — the passings and comings of life. First accept that, eventually, this moment of struggle will pass. Then, rather than focus on the agonizingly slow passage of each minute, strive to see the opportunity that can come out of your crisis — look for the coming in the passing.

Aeschylus once said, "By suffering comes wisdom." What can you learn from your experience? Reflect upon the source of your suffering, take stock of your life, and then set a new goal.

Nature teaches every living thing that it must adjust to life's changes, must learn how to harmonize with the passings and comings, must strive to be flexible. For centuries the Chinese have regarded bamboo as such a symbol of flexibility. For despite its hollowness, bamboo is strong enough to bend with the wind but flexible enough not to break.

You, too, must be as strong and flexible while you suffer. You must believe in the expression "No pain, no gain" to remind yourself that suffering is a normal part of growth. And you must be willing to look beyond your dilemma — to throw off the blinders that keep you focused on yourself and how terrible you feel.

Anne Frank wrote in her diary, "The best remedy for those who are afraid, lonely, or unhappy is to go outside, somewhere where they can be quite alone with the heavens, nature, and God. Because only then does one feel that all is as it should be and that God wishes to see people happy, amidst the simple beauty of nature. As long as this exists, and it certainly always will, I know that then there will always be comfort for every sorrow, whatever the circumstances may be."

So remember to go outside, where you can benefit from the stimulation provided by an outside environment. The brightness of the day, the expanse of the sky above you, the smells of the outside world, the sounds of humanity and nature, the absence of limiting doors and walls, your ability to move around, and being able to breathe deeply of the fresh air can all help to keep your spirits raised and your troubles in proportion. Look outside yourself, and what is inside will soon be healed.

Cooperation

"Cooperation with others.
Perception, experience, tenacity.
Know when to lead and when to follow."

— Tao Tze Ching

In businesses, fellowships, organizations, families, and other collectives the best leader is often the one who can motivate the others to achieve a common goal so that all the members of the group believe, once the aim is accomplished, that they've done the work together. Because of this, the best leader knows when to act, when to be passive, when others are receptive, and when others won't listen. The best leader, therefore, is the one who presents himself or herself as an equal to others — neither oppressively leading nor passively following, capable of rolling up sleeves and digging in to do whatever work needs to be done —

despite established "roles" or job titles — always ready to give praise and reluctant to criticize or judge, and skilled at building cooperation by exhibiting cooperation. Conductor Carlo Maria Giulini agrees, "My intention [as a conductor] has always been to arrive at human contact without enforcing authority. A musician, after all, is not a military officer. What matters most is human contact. The great mystery of music making requires real friendship among those who work together. Every member of the orchestra knows I am with him and her in my heart."

In nature, despite continual competition for food, water, shelter, and

survival, there's also a good amount of cooperative spirit that's exhibited. Geese that fly in formation, for example, follow their "flight leader" until the leader drops back from the point of the "V," at which time another goose will automatically take its place without causing the group to fall apart. Male and female "parents" will cooperate with one another to raise their young, each taking turns incubating the eggs and protecting the nest and searching for food. Apes, gorillas, and chimpanzees will cooperatively groom one another.

As well, cooperative hunting is exhibited by many species of carnivorous animals. Sometimes group hunting succeeds for the good of all members of the group, for the cooperation within the group allows the predators to surround or concentrate prey in one area to prevent escape and thereby ensure a kill that'll nourish all group members. Together, for example, dusky dolphins herd anchovies into the open ocean by diving and swimming at them from below and all sides while vocalizing loudly. The resulting tight ball of anchovies is then "served" to one dolphin at a time; each one takes a turn swimming into the mass of fish and taking some of the food while the other dolphins continue to maintain the herd of anchovies so others may eat.

Such cooperative hunting is evidenced with other species, too. Hawks and eagles display some division of labor and simple coordinative signaling in order to engage in effective teamwork when hunting such prey as cottontail rabbits and jackrabbits. The birds use a "flush-and-ambush" strategy; after spotting the prey, one bird swoops down in an attempt to penetrate the cover where the prey has hidden while one or more of the perched birds pounce to make the kill.

Some animals take advantage of cooperation in hunting in order to take a very large prey that couldn't be captured by a single predator. A group of South American giant otters, for example, can kill a large anaconda several times a single otter's size and weight. Other animals, such as lionesses, routinely hunt together, forming a sort of "tag team," where one or two lionesses may sit in full view of a herd of wildebeest, while another slinks towards the group on her belly to position herself near the middle of the herd to split it, and still another then suddenly charges the herd, scattering them about. The four lionesses are then in good positions to cut off at least one of the fleeing wildebeest for all to share.

Cooperation within nature happens in a multitude of other ways: a gentle summer rain provides water for green living things; a receding tide exposes food for gulls; dead leaves drop around a tree, slowly decay, and provide the tree with a rich source of nourishment. What you learn from such cooperation is that each element in nature becomes an integral, organic part of the overall "organization" of nature; each influences nature collectively and helps to shape it in some way by this influence.

So, too, can you learn to recognize your part in a great many "organizations" in your life — from your families to your work to your community associations to your environment. From this learning, you can then actively cultivate a cooperative spirit within the group to exert a subtle influence on others that will benefit each member of the group in positive ways.

Joy

*"Magic birds were dancing in the mystic marsh.
The grass swayed with them, and the shallow waters, and
the earth fluttered under them. The earth was dancing with
the cranes, and the low sun, and the wind and sky."*

— writer Marjorie Kinnan Rawlings

There's a story of a religious teacher whose daily sermons were wonderful and inspiring, and he often spent hours preparing them. He thought that someday he might collect them into a book and seek a publisher or even appear on his own cable television show. With such outcomes in the back of his mind, he was about to begin his sermon one day when a little bird came and sat on the window sill. It began to sing, and sang away with a joyful heart. Then it stopped and flew away. The teacher thought for a moment, folded the pages to his prepared sermon, and announced, "The sermon for this morning is over."

Joy is most often a wonderful surprise — totally unexpected, and yet never undesired. You may spend most of your life struggling to achieve some level of happiness and think, when you're happy, that you're also joyful, but happiness and joyfulness are two different emotions. Happiness is an outcome, a byproduct, from effort that you've exerted to achieve a goal, to realize a dream, to fulfill a desire. Happiness springs from things — a job promotion, a vacation, a kiss, walking with your dog, getting out of financial debt, eating a delicious meal, spending time with a friend.

But joy is a gift that's given to you even when it's not your birthday, a holiday, or an anniversary. Joy happens simply because joy *is*. As J. Ruth Gendler writes in *The Book of Qualities*, "[Joy] is in love with life, all of it, the sun and the rain and the rainbow. She rides horses at Half Moon Bay under the October moon. She climbs mountains. She sings in hills. She jumps from hot spring to the cold stream without hesitation."

Joy is spontaneous; it's a butterfly that suddenly alights on your arm or a hummingbird that flits quickly in and out of your view. Joy is playful; it's two chipmunks engaged in a lively game of hide-and-seek on a stone wall, or puppies pouncing and tumbling together. Joy is lighthearted; it's peepers participating in an endless communication with the night or a duck paddling gracefully around a pond. Joy is lively; it's a brook racing a slalom course down the side of a hill, spilling over rocks and ducking under sticks, or a field mouse scampering in a field of wheat, nosing about for tasty kernals. Joy is one with the moment; it's a cat stretching in a patch of sunlight or a bee buzzing non-stop from flower to flower.

Joy ought never to be desired as a goal; you can't find joy by simply deciding, "Today I'll be more joyful."

Joy ought never to be a conditional aspect of your life; it's unrealistic to expect that you'll feel joy once you get a raise or the coveted corner office. And joy ought never to be an expected outcome for things that are sought after, worked hard for, or struggled over. There's much that you can expect to gain from such efforts — financial security, intellectual stimulation, or satisfaction of a physical or emotional need. But joy ought not to be considered as a gain, for joy simply exists. Search for it, and you'll never find it. Yet pay no attention to it, and it will be there, right by your side.

Have you ever observed squirrels in your backyard or in a nearby park? With their boundless energy, they seem to be on a never-ending mission of joyous union with life. They scurry up and down tree trunks, hang from branches, leap gracefully from tree top to tree top, and then jump down to the ground. There they locate nuts and other edibles and either bury them as a dog would bury a bone for future snacking or furiously nibble at the food. Sometimes, in mid-meal, they dart off once again — this time, perhaps, to greet another squirrel, roll playfully on the grass together, then chase each other around and around the base of a tree trunk.

Squirrels are like individualized packets of joy. Everything they do seems to give them pleasure: walking across telephone wires like circus acrobats, jumping from tree to tree, wiggling their noses, scampering about, and swishing their long, bushy tails. What the squirrels capture is a joy of life — a happiness in being alive and having many enjoyable things to do from the moment they wake up to the time they need rest.

Nature teaches you not to take yourself or life too seriously. Nature teaches you to laugh and play more. Nature teaches you to focus less on answers and solutions and more on the things that bring you pleasure. Nature teaches you to welcome joy when joy comes to you. As a Chinese proverb states, "A bird does not sing because it has an answer — it sings because it has a song." From this moment on, discover the joy in life you can experience through the simple act of singing your own song.

Liberation

"The elemental simplicities of wilderness travel were thrills not because of their novelty, but because they represented complete freedom to make mistakes. The wilderness gave them their first taste of those rewards and penalties for wise and foolish acts which every woodsman faces daily, but against which civilization has built a thousand buffers."

— writer and naturalist Aldo Leopold

Do you realize that day after day, you're being held prisoner by a most unforgiving and relentlessly driven jailer — yourself? You, as a jailer, can be quite unfair to you, as a prisoner. It's almost as if you're at constant war with yourself, battling through day after day of competition, confrontation, and mounting frustration while, at the same time, you're driven by a fear that not only are you not "good enough," but you'll never — ever — be good enough. You, as prisoner, have your own ideals of who you are, what you'd like to be doing, and where you'd like to be going in your life but you, as a jailer, contradict such ideals with visions of who you ought to be, what you ought to be doing, and where you ought to be going in your life.

Imagine what it would be like if you were alone in the wilderness for a few days and applied the same kind of restrictive thinking to needing to survive in nature on your own. You might want to gather up firewood as quickly as you can and start a warming fire, but instead spend hours shivering because you feel you ought to collect just the right wood to build just the right fire. Your hunger might grow because you feel you ought not to eat anything that isn't shrink-wrapped, prepared in a proper manner, or "dirty." The rain, the wind, and other

elements might penetrate clothing you wore — clothes you felt you ought to wear "out in the wild." Boredom might overwhelm you because you can't decide what you ought to be doing and so, instead, you opt to do nothing.

When you're not at peace with yourself, you're not a free person. When you're not at peace with yourself, you're held captive by the bonds of shoulds and oughts. When you're not at peace with yourself, you're restricted from living life to the fullest. When you're not at peace with yourself, you're trapped in a life that's filled with stress, strife, and struggle. When you're not at peace with yourself, you're held down, powerless, limited, dominated, and weakened by the standards, dreams, goals, desires, and paths that others have created for you. Think about your relationships, your career, your family, your physical appearance, your finances, where you live. If you're not at peace with such things, then you're probably not at peace with yourself.

To find such peace, you need to stop struggling to free yourself. For the moment you stop struggling, you're free. To illustrate this, one day a robin mistakenly flew into an apartment through open sliding glass doors. Confused and frightened by its confining new environment, the distressed bird frantically fluttered about the living room, banging into walls and hitting the ceiling. In a panic, it repeatedly hurled itself against the windows and screens in an effort to get out.

Finally, exhausted and dazed, it perched on the back of a chair. As the small creature panted through its wide-open beak, it suddenly cocked its head to the side. It listened to the sounds of other birds coming from outside the open glass doors. It hopped down from the chair, fluttered across the floor to the doors, then quickly flew outside to a nearby tree branch, where it soon began to sing.

In nature, liberation comes to its living things when they, on their own, are able to find the "open doors" that will release them from their confinement. Nature's living things work with the conflicts and changes in their environment so they can continue to quickly and easily resolve their problems.

You, too, can open the doors to your own, self-imposed cell and spring free by recognizing that life has many options. If you can be creative, resourceful, and respect yourself and what you want and need, then you can be free to pursue the options of life. You don't have to do what others want you to do all or even most of the time. You don't have to do things perfectly, either. You don't have to have the ideal body. You don't have to be the wonderful son or daughter or be the most romantic partner. You can make mistakes. You can do silly, foolish things. You can act on impulses. You can be free!

Learn to live by the words of writer Jack London, who declared with determination, "I would rather be ashes than dust! I would rather my sparks should burn out in a blaze than it should be stifled by dry-rot. I would rather be a superb meteor, every atom of me in magnificent glow, than asleep and permanent as a planet. The proper function of man is to live, not to exist. I shall not waste my days trying to prolong them. I shall use my time."

Perseverance

"The difference between perserverance and obstinacy is that one comes from a strong will and the other from a strong won't."

— Henry Ward Beecher

To get the most out of life, you need to put effort into it. You've probably heard the phrase many times before — you don't get something for nothing. It's only when you're willing to try, to do, to dare, to risk, and to be persistent that you're rewarded by getting something out of your doing. But in order to get, you have to give; you need to expend energy.

A good example of this type of reward-based perseverance comes from birds. Birds rely primarily on vision to locate and capture food, but how they then eat what they've caught can require a high level of ingenuity and persistence. Herring gulls and crows, for instance,

eat clams, whelks, and other shellfish; they have to employ enterprising behaviors not only to locate this food, but also to break through the outer shells to get at the food.

As the bird flies, it must first look down and be able to recognize something that's edible after its outer shell is broken. Then the bird must swoop down, pick it up, fly with it to a suitable location, and drop it from a sufficient height on a hard enough surface that'll cause the shell to break. The majority of shells the bird recovers are often dropped on rocks, roads, parking lots, and sea walls. But the shells don't always break on the first

attempt, necessitating that the bird swoop down once again to pick up the unbroken shell and drop it.

A particular population of crows that nests on an island near the coast of British Columbia was observed by researchers, who tracked the birds' habit of gathering whelks at low tide and dropping them on particularly rocky areas. The crows dropped the whelks from heights of three to eight meters, but only about one in four drops broke the shell. Many unbroken shells had to be picked up and dropped over and over again.

Unless they were disturbed during this time, the crows persisted in the retrieval-and-drop process until the shell finally broke; sometimes it took as many as twenty drops before the shells cracked and the soft parts could be eaten.

While flying higher and dropping the shell from a greater height might have caused the shell to break much quicker, the birds rarely flew higher. One reason for that might have been the birds' vision restriction. But since the crows sometimes dipped broken whelks into freshwater pools before eating them, the birds may have been trying to make it easier to eat the contents of the shell by gently breaking the shell rather than by shattering it.

How many times have you exhibited similar perseverance in your life, choosing to do something over and over again until you earned your anticipated reward? Never giving up, despite the odds or obstacles, is not only a test of belief in yourself and what you can do, but is also a symbol of how you approach life. When confronted by impending defeat, failure, disappointment, frustration, or rejection, it may be far easier to simply give up after one, two, or only a few tries. But such an action can shape the attitude you then bring into every situation of your life. And that attitude can spell the difference between long-term success and satisfaction or a series of defeats.

How much like the crow can you be in your life? Can you learn to develop the same level of perseverance in all the things you do? When Thomas Edison's manufacturing facilites were heavily damaged by fire in 1914, Edison lost nearly one million dollars worth of equipment and all the records he had kept. But the next morning, as the inventor surveyed the charred embers, he said, "There is value in disaster. All our mistakes are burned up. Now we can start anew." Imagine what your world would be like today if Edison hadn't continued his work after the fire. His positive approach to personal disaster reflected a "can-do" philosophy rather than a "can't-do" one.

An American proverb advises, "Chop your own wood and it will warm you twice." Nature, too, teaches you that such perseverance has its rewards, but only if you're able to give your full effort to whatever you do. Like chopping wood, when you expend energy you'll be rewarded.

Nourishment

*"... And He said: This is a beautiful world
that I have given you.
Take good care of it; do not ruin it."*

— Jewish prayer

In the past, feasting was a way to establish a sense of community and then bind that community closer together. While the food was an important reason for people to come together, because food was often scarce and the people badly needed the physical nourishment, the sharing with one another in a gathering was also important, for it affirmed or reaffirmed a valuable sense of belonging and connection with one another; this was what gave back sustenance to the soul.

Nourishment can be thought of as more than the food and water you need to stay healthy and alive. What you share with every living creature is the need to satisfy more than just your hunger. Your intellect needs to be nourished as well, through education and experience. Your emotions need to be nourished, too, through communication, expression, and the development of love and passion. And your faith needs to be nourished through prayer and meditation.

Harmony with humanity means being able to be a separate individual — to nourish yourself — as well as to be someone who can connect with the diversity of many individuals — to nourish a community. The Omaha Indian tribe had a saying, "The bird who has eaten cannot fly with the bird that is hungry"; what that means is that it's easier to cooperate, resolve conflicts, and to interact in peaceful harmony when you're linked with others who think, feel, act, and believe in similar ways or who are banded together for a common purpose. It becomes much harder when you're divided by who each of you are individually and by each set of wants and needs.

It's a well-known fact that once a single foraging worker bee has discovered a rich source of food, such as flowers that may have just come into bloom, it communicates with other bees from the same colony so that within a matter of minutes the entire colony can benefit from the food source found by one. This is the essence of a nourishing and rewarding community. Life without such community can be both unhealthy and unhappy; research has shown that constant interaction with strangers in crowded cities makes people depressed; as well, there are many species of living things that would die if they didn't live and grow within a community. So life that's lived within a community creates a healthier world both personally — for each member of the group — and ecologically — for the world at large.

Laurel's Kitchen, a natural foods cookbook, provides a recipe for such a healthier world: "Suppose we were to commit ourselves to building up a *neighborhood* where we live: a kind of village where lives overlap and intermingle in a rich and productive way? What greater challenge to our creativity? Loneliness comes whenever we dwell on ourselves, and it leaves immediately once we start working for the welfare of others, beginning with those immediately around us."

You can create a nourishing community within your family of origin or an extended family, with those who live in your apartment building or in the neighborhood, or in a social, civic, or religious organization. Share rides with one another. Borrow eggs and cups of sugar, and be willing to lend tools. Swap homegrown vegetables or start a community garden. Share children's used toys and clothing. Get together for pot-luck dinners. Provide services for one another as a way of saving money; the beautician can give a haircut to the mechanic in exchange for a car tune-up.

Then extend your community outward; reach out to others in need as a group a few times a year. Collect food and clothing for food pantries and charitable organizations. Donate blood.

Volunteer to prepare or serve food during a holiday at a soup kitchen or shelter. Start and maintain a read-aloud program for children at the local library. Deliver meals to shut-ins. Shovel paths and driveways for others. Establish a phone tree for latch-key kids.

As well, support your natural community. Learn about your local wildlife. Put up bluebird houses in local fields. Plant a tree. Establish a backyard habitat, complete with a freshwater source. Provide food supplements such as suet and peanuts during harsh weather, nesting boxes or birdhouses, and shrubs and trees for protection from weather and predators.

By cooperating with humanity and nature, you're affirming the essential bonds that nourish all living things. For, as the Metea Indians once said, "Our country was given us by the Great Spirit, who gave it to us to hunt upon, to make our cornfields upon, to live upon, to make our beds upon when we die."

Synchronicity

"The sky is round, and I have heard that the earth is round like a ball, and so are all the stars. The wind, in its greatest power, whirls. Birds make their nests in circles, for theirs is the same religion as ours.... Even the seasons form a great circle in their changing, and always come again to where they were."

— Lakota Sioux holy man Black Elk

Do you know that native palm trees grow in Arizona — not on the desert, but on the shady side of a mountain? Jutting majestically out from the granite sides of a 2500-foot canyon in the Kofa Mountains of Arizona are the only native palm trees in the entire state. How do the tropical plants live year after year in the dark, almost perpendicular sides of the narrow gorge? How can they flourish when the sun reaches them only two hours in a day? Botanists who have studied this incredible phenomenon have concluded that the stone walls of the canyon reflect enough light and store enough warmth throughout the day to enable the trees to survive in the

seemingly uninhabitable environment. Thus, it isn't an oddity of nature or mere coincidence that the trees happen to grow out of those particular canyon walls; rather, there's a supportive relationship that has been created between the environment of the canyon walls and the needs of the palm trees that allows the trees to grow.

Such synchronicity often occurs in nature; day-to-day examples abound. A dry spell is followed by a much-needed rain. Oak trees release bumper crops of acorns right before a severe winter, which provides ample food for winter wildlife. Gentle breezes nudge seeds from plants so the seeds

can fall to the ground and sprout. Bees unknowingly gather pollen and cross-pollinate flowers. Earthworms excrete valuable nitrogen into the ground as well as aerate the soil.

What sometimes may seem to be mere coincidences in your life may actually be meaningfully related. Think of how you met your life partner, what made you decide to attend the college you did, how you found your current job, why you're living where you are right now. Then think about the little things that happen each day in your life that end up with surprisingly meaningful outcomes — how you might have left for work at a different time one morning and ended up bumping into a childhood friend while standing in line for coffee, how you might have been thinking about your sibling on the same day a card arrived from her in the mail, or how sitting next to someone at a busy lunch counter resulted in a job offer.

You may think that such things are really examples of blind luck rather than some synchronatic "grand plan." For, as scientist Lewis Thomas once commented, "Statistically, the probability of any one of us being here is so small that you'd think the mere fact of existing would keep us all in a contented dazzlement of surprise." Yet was it blind luck or synchronicity that led to the start of life on Earth about four billion years ago? Somehow the precursor molecules of life fashioned themselves into a reproduceable arrangement that kept reappearing even after repeated bombardments of the planet by huge comets and asteroids. Countless reproductions and sexual interweavings resulted in the species Homo sapiens, and two members of that species happened to end up as your parents.

Now think: What were the odds of your parents meeting? Or, for that matter, not meeting? Would you be here if they hadn't met? Or, if the one out of five million gene-carrying spermatozoa that penetrated your mother's egg didn't enter the egg — but a different sperm did — would you be someone who's totally different? The odds of you being alive are so infinitesimally small that it's hard to imagine that mere coincidence or blind luck is how life has evolved and continues to evolve on Earth. Think about it. Certainly the world today would be a much different place to live in if dinosaurs had survived. But, while dinosaurs were evolving into huge, efficient, and powerful creatures, mammals remained relatively small. Because mammals required less food to stay alive and were furry and warm-blooded, they were more adaptable to the ensuing drastic changes in temperature and periods of darkness that enveloped the planet — circumstances that the dinosaurs couldn't adapt to, thereby leaving a vacant ecological niche that the mammals easily filled. To imagine that such things were mere coincidences would mean that there was no meaningful purpose to life. But how, then, could evolution of man and so many other living things occur unless each event that had happened throughout the history of the planet transformed the Earth into a more inhabitable environment for them?

If you believe in synchronicity rather than luck and happenstance, then you'll believe in the words of Anne Morrow Lindbergh, who writes, "... each cycle of the tide is valid; each cycle of the wave is valid; each cycle of a relationship is valid." In day-to-day living, everything is meaningful.

Pace

"If a man does not keep pace with his companions, perhaps it is because he hears a different drummer. Let him step to the music he hears, however measured or far away."

— Henry David Thoreau

The belief in yin and yang life force is central to Eastern philosophy. This philosophy explains that yin is a phrase of repose and relaxation, while yang is the phase of activity. All of life emerges from the harmonious synthesis of these two life forces. You need both moments of reflection and introspection for your actions to have purpose and meaning, as well as moments of action so your thoughts can take form.

Western philosophy, on the other hand, proposes a choice: action or repose. Most Americans prefer yang over yin, as evidenced through acceptance of the Puritan work ethic, by constantly burning the candle at both ends, and by equating a successful day with the quantity — not the quality — of tasks completed. Thoreau aptly illustrated this yang ethic — this unnatural drive — in one of his journal entries: "If a man walk in the woods for love of them half of each day, he is in danger of being regarded as a loafer; but if he spends his whole day as a speculator, shearing off those woods and making earth bald before her time, he is esteemed an industrious and enterprising citizen."

Yet without a balance of yin and yang in your life, you'll find it hard to learn how to pace yourself; you'll go from times of overwork to periods of exhaustion and collapse. No living

thing, other than man, does this to itself; no living thing, other than man, makes a conscious choice between yin and yang; no living thing, other than man, is incapable of balancing active time with inactive time; no living thing, other than man, feels guilty during the natural cycle of rest, relaxation, and rejuvenation.

Nature teaches you that life is naturally made up of dynamic polarities — day and night, hot and cold, summer and winter, ebb and flow, excess and scarcity, valley and mountain, heaven and Earth. So, too, is your life made up of dynamic polarities — work and play, rest and exercise, socializing and introspection, thinking and feeling, nurturing and achieving, speaking and listening, reasoning and intuiting, action and repose. While nature teaches that all of life embodies yin and embraces yang, what your life may reveal is that you repeatedly become stuck in one extreme or the other. Sometimes you may be too yin, living life in a state of inactivity as you procrastinate and put off things that need your time and attention; sometimes you may be too yang, living life like a whirling dervish, in perpetual motion.

To restore your balance, you need to alter your pace so that you're not operating at one speed — high or low — for a majority of the time. You need to be able to downshift your gears as easily as you can speed up. You need to be more aware of the natural patterns in life so you can learn to flow with them.

What all this means is that you need to accept that there will always be times of intense activity in your life — deadlines that need to be met; kids who need to get fed, dressed, and out the door; housework that needs to get done; plans that need to be made. But you also need to accept that there are going to have to be times in your life in which you slow the pace down — times when you can be quiet, peaceful, and reflective so that you can recharge your depleted energy.

Although all living things, other than man, know how to naturally do this, altering your pace may not come naturally at first. You may have to set aside time each day in which you "decompress," unwind, settle back, take a deep breath, close your eyes, soak in a hot tub, listen to soothing music, or do whatever you need to do to force yourself to shift from yang to yin.

It may help if you think of yourself as a mountain climber. To get up the mountain, you need to be yang — you need to exert hard, steady, aerobic effort. But then, at some point, your muscles will begin to ache, your pace will slow down, your breathing will become labored, and you'll need to be yin. Climb, bivouac, climb, bivouac. Go fast, go slow. That is how you need to live your life.

Allow time in your yang schedule for yin. Or else you're sure to end up, as Bess Streeter Aldrich described in *Spring Came on Forever*, "…like the little moles under the earth carrying out blindly the work of digging, thinking our own dark passage-ways constitute all there is to the world."

31

Growth

"Flowing water never grows stagnant."

— Tao Tze Ching

Nothing in nature ever stops growing. Even in the winter, there's always a dawning nature in what appears to be the sunset of life for many living things. Take the sugar maple trees, for instance. Sometime in late February or early March, when the weather achieves a perilous balance between winter and spring — when it's cold at night and warm during the day — the trees begin to activate for spring. As the weather warms up, the sap in the trees expels carbon dioxide, which forms bubbles. The bubbling, expanding carbon dioxide puts pressure on the vessels that conduct the sap; the pressure drives the sap upward and downward, flowing within the tree. Severing the vessels with a taphole diverts the flow of sap into the waiting sap bucket; it takes about forty gallons of sap just to make one gallon of syrup.

If the weather stays warm for awhile, the sap stops running. But if the cold weather returns, the tree recharges itself and re-enters a sap-producing cycle. So while you may think that the sugar maples — as well as much of nature — depend upon the warmth of spring and summer in order to grow, in reality it's the waning times of autumn and winter in which nature assists continued growth or ensures new growth each coming season.

A prime example of nature's continued growth is ensured by the leaves trees shed in autumn. While you may view the cascade of leaves to the ground with dread because the massive shedding signals upcoming weekends of hard labor in your backyard with a rake, each leaf is critical to the continued growth of life in woodland streams. When the leaves drop into the water or are blown in by the chill autumn winds, they become soaked. After immersion, they provide an abundance of organic carbon — a substance that's found in anything that was once alive — for aquatic insects and crustaceans known as "shredders." The shredders literally shred the leaves and other dead plant life, further breaking down the rich source of carbon that's fed into the water; as well, the nourished shredders themselves become a prime food source for trout and other fish in the stream.

Growth in your life, as in nature, also comes from the natural process of maturing through the seasons of your life. Each day, as you grow older, you're in a constant state of growth from the personal changes you make, the risks you take, the challenges you face, the decisions you make, the people you meet, the gains you make, the setbacks you suffer, the illnesses and injuries you heal and grow stronger from, the new experiences you have. Give up your growth, and your muscles, your mind, and your spirit will atrophy and die: Your muscles won't strengthen without exercise, your intellect won't sharpen without thinking and learning, and your spirit won't soar without something to excite it. So you must continue to grow.

Nature teaches you to grow through all the seasons of your life — spring, summer, autumn, and winter. While nothing can reverse the natural progression of the years, you can use each season wisely, choosing to grow as much as you can. Treat each day as a new and exciting step in your growth. Live by the words of the Cherokees, who believed in everlasting life and growth: "... it is coming quickly," they said when nature was about to make a change. "A subtle greening has begun in sheltered places. The wild rose canes laid flat by cold winter winds are no longer gray. Purple striped dayflowers and tiny four-petal blue-eyes bloom profusely with a minimum of sunlight and warm air. The wild strawberry has put out new leaves, and we see the eternal miracle that never grows old — the new baby calf."

Spring is never far away in your life when you can live through each winter. Begin now to prepare for the new growth that awaits you. No matter how old you are, keep exercising all parts of yourself. Then you'll never grow stagnant.

Support

"I have learned the depths of strength and trust that are present in me and my fellow man. I shall try to remember that any of my neighbors or fellow workers could have belayed the climbing rope for me or given me his hand when I was slipping off a steep slope. I may forget, but I will try to remember."

— an Outward Bound student

There's a story told about a king who suddenly awakens in the middle of the night and summons the kingdom's wisest seer into his bedchambers. "Oh, Great Seer," the king says, "my sleep is troubled for I do not know the answer to this question: What is holding up the earth?"

"Your majesty," replies the seer, "the earth rests on the back of a giant elephant."

The king sighs in relief, and then goes back to sleep. But it isn't long before he awakens in a cold sweat and once again summons the seer to his bedchambers. "Tell me, Great Seer," the king says, "what is holding up the elephant?"

The seer replies, "The elephant stands on the back of a giant turtle."

The king sighs again, reaches for his bed candle to blow out the flame, and then stops. "But Seer..." the king begins.

The seer holds up his hand. "You can stop right there, your Majesty," he says. "It's turtles all the way down."

Nature supports all of its living things; no one thing could ever live successfully on its own without the support of other living things. Every living thing, for example, needs the earth, needs water, and needs the air. As well, most every living thing needs other living things for sustenance and to ensure its continued growth.

Because of this supportive network of living things, all of creation can be seen as

interdependent. What this means is that you may often find yourself in the position — not always by chance and sometimes by design — to involve yourself in many different ways in the world around you. Within the context of your home, your job, your partner, your family, your friends, your environment, and others with whom you have contact, there are hundreds of experiences that create opportunities for you to reach out to others, to support them in some way, to make yourself necessary to them.

How can you be necessary? Think of how a tree is necessary to you. On a hot day, its cooling shade gives you relief from the sun. So, too, can you provide relief and comfort to others who share your journey through life. A tree is essential in controlling the erosion of topsoil; its root systems not only help hold the soil in place, but also absorb runoff that would wash the soil away. So, too, can you support others during times of stress and strife, to help hold them in place, to give them strength so they can get through their difficult times. A tree provides products such as lumber, pulp for paper, turpentine, sap for syrup, nuts, fruit, and medicines. So, too, can you provide "products" that will benefit others; the

efforts and talents you show others can provide them with creative inspiration and motivation they can use to help them to discover their own talents and abilities. Finally, a tree, even in death, is still an essential part of nature; its rotting trunk provides homes for many creatures and the decaying process provides rich nutrients for the soil. So, too, can you offer the lessons you've learned from life as "shelter" for others so they can benefit from the richness of your experiences.

Because every person is necessary to the completion of your existence — and because you're also necessary to theirs — nature teaches you that you need to extend yourself to others. Each day you must make yourself necessary to others. Be there for them and be grateful for their existence in your life.

Edward Abbey once wrote, "How strange and wonderful is our home, our earth, with its swirling vaporous atmosphere, its flowing and frozen liquids, its trembling plants, its creeping, crawling, climbing creatures, the croaking things with wings that hang on rocks and soar through the fog, the furry grass, the scaly seas." It is all here, each aspect of life — you and every living thing — and it's imperative that you support one another.

Detachment

"When I gaze into the stars, they look down upon me with pity from their serene and silent spaces, like eyes glistening with tears over the little lot of man. Thousands of generations, all as noisy as our own, have been swallowed up by time, and there remains no record of them any more. Yet Acturus and Orion, Sirius and Pleiades, are still shining in their courses, clear and young, as when the shepherd first noted them in the plain of Shinar!"

— Scottish historian and essayist Thomas Carlyle

Can you imagine what it would be like if you not only had to move every year, but either had to find an unoccupied living space before bad weather set in or had to build your own shelter from whatever scrap materials you could find? Can you imagine how difficult it would be to have to hunt or forage for your food every day, from sunup to sundown? Can you imagine how unsettling it might be to live in fear for your life each day, never knowing when you might become the next meal for another living creature? Can you imagine how helpless you might feel if there were no painkillers to anesthetize your pain, no doctors to treat your wounds and injuries, and no bandages or ointments to stop your bleeding?

But can you also imagine what it would be like to have no possessions, no need for money, no job pressures, no rules to live by, no taxes to file, no long commutes, no one nagging or pestering you, no time clock, no crime and no punishment, no measurements, no constraints? French writer and philosopher Voltaire once pointed out that "Animals have a prodigious advantage over us: they foresee neither evils nor death." Because of this, animals — as well as all living things — know how to be detached from the things human beings are quite attached to. All living things

accept the fluidity of life and its change-ability; they know how to adapt because they must adapt. While some living things may zealously guard food, shelter, a mate, their young, and their territory, such behavior doesn't suggest attachment to such things but rather the necessity for survival of themselves as well as their species.

Yet human beings can become so attached to even the smallest of things — a pair of basketball sneakers — that they would kill another human being just to get the shoes. Human beings can become so attached to dead-end, unfulfilling jobs or abusive relationships that even when their health and well-being are in jeopardy, they won't leave. Human beings can become so attached to people, to drugs, to alcohol, to the pursuit of money, to a posh address, to living a glamorous lifestyle, and to so many other people, places, or things that they would risk living in constant stress and even forget to take care of themselves.

The downside to such obsessive human attachment, according to spiritualist Shakti Gawain, is that "It's easy to lose our focus, to get lost in other people, external goals, and desires... we lose our connection to the universe inside ourselves. As long as we focus on the outside there will always be an empty, hungry, lost place inside that needs to be filled."

As in nature, being detached means caring without getting caught up in day-to-day commotions. Living things awaken to the world each day without creating checklists of things to do, without running themselves into a frenzy over the welfare of others, or without making themselves into nervous wrecks as they struggle to attain more and more. As well, living things can make peace with the world each night without tossing and turning over all the things that have been left undone, without being racked with guilt and worry over how others are doing, and without pondering how to make their stockpiles even bigger.

Nature teaches us the benefits of detachment — in being able to participate in life's changing panorama with patience, acceptance, and a positive attitude; in being able to focus on oneself not in selfish ways, but in self-caring, self-nurturing, and self-protecting ways; in being able to give compassionate support to others while, at the same time, showing them respect for their right to find their own way; in being able to be less judgmental and critical of others in order to connect with them in emotionally beneficial ways; in being able to be liberated from the fear of letting others down in order to live in greater harmony with the world; and in being able to reconnect with and become part of the universe — a universe in which, according to Swedish diplomat and humanitarian Dag Hammarskjöld "... man is no longer the center of the world, only a witness, but a witness who is also a partner in the silent life of nature, bound by secret affinities to the trees."

Acceptance

"You must travel the river, live on it, follow it when there is morning light, and follow it when there is nothing but dark and the banks have blurred into shadows."

— Wil Haygood

Have you ever tried to swim against a current? Even though the safety of shore may be only yards away, the pull of the current may be so strong that you may panic or exhaust yourself in your efforts to go a short distance.

But what happens if you simply relax and go with the flow of the current? While you may drift further down from where you'd ideally like to be, you eventually are able to leave the water without your energy depleted or your peace of mind disrupted.

Can you travel the river of your life by accepting the way things happen, or do you constantly battle against the current, trying to force changes in people, places, or things, by overreacting to situations that are out of your control, or by trying to force yourself to do things you're simply not capable of doing? One way — going with the flow — allows you to drift calmly and contentedly as well as helps foster a healthy, objective perspective about all the circumstances and events in life; the other way leaves you weary, disrupted, and disturbed.

"Going with the flow" is an appropriate symbol for acceptance, for acceptance is acting within the framework of a circumstance. All around you, there are countless examples of such acceptance in nature. For example, if the countryside is gripped in drought, thirsty plants don't become agitated and toss curses at the sky. Rather, they accept their fate, live in the uncomfortable state — without complaint — for as long as they can, and oftentimes work within the framework of their circumstance to try to effect positive change. For instance, a thirsty plant could send new shoots upward from its roots in order to take advantage of any light rain that might fall or to be ready to adsorb whatever moisture it can from the early morning dew.

Acceptance is not about fatalism, about being helpless or hopeless, about giving up in any way, or about being stagnant or inactive. It's about being sensible as well as being able to take correct action at the appropriate time. So if you're the farmer who's experiencing the drought, you know to prepare for such a circumstance by storing water or by sparingly using the water you've stored to nourish your crop. You know not to plant anything that requires a lot of water — flowers, for instance, which have to be watered every day. You know that to cry out in anger or frustration won't make the rain fall, so you don't waste your time with such actions.

To work with fate has always been nature's lesson for humankind. Sometimes fate has been out of the control of human influence — a drought, for instance — but sometimes fate has been in the control of humans — by the planned diversion of water to another source, for example, which then deprives an area of its life-giving water. Yet nature accepts all that it's given, both natural and unnatural, by going with the flow and continuing to do what it needs to do in order to survive. As written in the book of Job 14:7–9:

> *"For there is hope for a tree,*
> *if it be cut down, that it will sprout again,*
> *and that its shoots will not cease.*
> *Though its root grow old in the earth,*
> *and its stump die in the ground,*
> *yet at the scent of water it will bud*
> *and put forth branches like a young plant."*

Acceptance is a dynamic, life-giving and life-affirming act. Acceptance is self-preservation. Acceptance is heightened activity — not necessarily to get one's way or to force a change — but to go about the business of preparation for the future, whether that future be the next few moments or the next few years. And acceptance is wisdom, in knowing when to withdraw to restore valuable energy and to regain strength. There's an old Chinese saying, "The tortoise is good at nurturing energy, so it can survive a century without food." Like the tortoise, humans can live to an advanced age by applying this valuable lesson in acceptance.

35 Energy

"Nature does not proceed by leaps."

— Swedish botanist Carolus Linnaeus

One summer night, a camp counselor was showing a group of campers how to cook a marshmallow over a campfire. "First you have to find a green stick and slide your marshmallow onto it," she directed. "Then you need to hold the stick a few inches above the fire, like so."

"For how long?" asked a camper. "How do you know when the marshmallow's done?"

"Well, that depends," answered the counselor. "You see, it's not ready now because it's only a light brown color." The counselor continued to hold the stick over the fire for a few seconds longer. "And it's not ready now because it's not quite a golden brown color." A few more seconds passed. "And it's not ready now because it hasn't started to puff up yet." A few more seconds passed. Then, suddenly, the marshmallow burst into flame. The counselor quickly pulled the stick out of the fire and frantically blew on the marshmallow.

"Is it done now?" asked the camper.

The counselor sighed and held up the smoking, blackened, oozing glob. "No. Now it's beyond done. It's ruined."

Humankind is quite skilled at keeping themselves "in the fire" for "just a few minutes more" each day — in the work fire, the errand-running fire, the chore fire, the caretaking fire, the holiday planning fire, the studying fire, the partying fire. Sometimes it's hard to avoid such "fire-fighting" duties; they may have become a "natural" part of your life. And, every once in a while, it's okay to spend a little more time being productive, being studious, being diligent, or being playful.

But when the fire alarms in your life go off time and again and you're never allowed to take a break, such actions can have a detrimental effect. Like the marshmallow that's been left too long over a hot flame, you can end up getting burned out pretty quickly. Your ability to respond efficiently and effectively, putting in your best effort each time, will gradually diminish. As well, your energy will soon be depleted unless you take a break. As the Sioux Indians advised, "One must learn from the bite of the fire to leave it alone."

Think of how differently you could feel if you were able to set limits in your life that kept you from getting burned out or feeling as if you're in a state of perpetual burnout. Imagine how you might handle things in your life if you were able to set limits rather than constantly force yourself to go beyond your limits. Imagine how differently you'd feel — physically, emotionally, and

spiritually — if you were able to say "Enough!" rather than "Just a few seconds more." Imagine what it would be like if, from now on, you could get to bed at a reasonable time each night so you could awaken refreshed and revitalized in the morning — the way nature's living things do.

The Chinese word *tzu jan* means "natural sciences" as well as "living in harmony with nature." When you're tuned in to the cycles of nature, you can be more sensitive to your energy flow. This means living in harmony with the natural seasons — spring, summer, winter, and fall — as well as living in harmony with your natural cycles. As in nature, you have cycles in your life when your energies go through renewal (spring), high output and drive (summer), decline (fall), and exhaustion (winter). Respecting these cycles means avoiding being driven and compulsive when you're not and refraining from exhausting yourself by pushing yourself beyond your capabilities. It means honoring your energies, not fighting them.

How can you do this? Sit or lie down in a comfortable position and close your eyes. In your mind, picture yourself walking down thickly carpeted stairs as you count slowly backwards from ten. With each step, imagine that you're descending into a lush forest glen just after the sun has set. When you reach the last step, look around you. Perhaps you see a sparkling stream that reflects a shimmering full moon. Maybe there are distant mountains capped by a night sky decorated with twinkling stars. Perhaps the gentle hoot of the owl, the low "grumps" of bull frogs, and the tender sounds of crickets fill the air.

Breathe deeply and trust that this vision shows you nature's wisdom in conserving and preserving the energy of all living things: that each day must wane into a welcome mellowness, a soothing smoothness, and a gently departed peace in order for each new day to dawn with a contagious happiness and great surges of fire-starting energies.

Problem-Solving

*"What would I discover about the cottonwoods
if when I walked to the mailbox I listened to them instead
of looked at them? What would I find out about
the rain if I didn't run inside?"*

— Hugh Prather

Five ravens that had been captured as nestlings were held in large outdoor cages until they were full-grown. The ravens had been fed for months with dead animals and other pieces of meat that had been tossed on the ground inside their cage. Then, one day, their caretakers hung a chunk of meat from one of the horizontal poles in the cage by a piece of string. At first the ravens flew at the suspended food, but they couldn't detach anything edible. Once in a while they also pulled at the string from the bottom of the cage to try to get closer to the food, but this method also failed to reward them with food.

Then, after several hours, one raven was observed to carry out a series of actions that brought the food within its reach and solved the problem. The raven reached down, grasped the string in its bill, and pulled it up. Then it held the slack string in one foot, released the string in its beak, and reached down again to grasp the string and pull it up. Each time it shifted its grasp on the string with its foot. It repeated this sequence four or five times until it obtained the meat.

While this experiment was done in a controlled setting, there are other evidences of problem-solving in nature that haven't had any human influence. Beavers are ingenious at plugging water leaks, for instance, sometimes cutting

pieces of wood to fit a particular hole through which water had been escaping. As well, in late winter some beavers cut holes in dams they previously constructed in order to cause the water level to drop so they can swim under the ice without holding their breath. Plovers not only carry out injury-simulating distraction displays that lead predators away from their eggs or young, they'll adjust such displays according to a predator's behavior. Chimpanzees have used rocks for centuries to smash open nuts that are too hard to open with hands or teeth; the sound of such nut-cracking led early European explorers to think that natives were forging metal tools somewhere in the depths of the rain forest. Green-backed herons will toss twigs into ponds to attract curious minnows, which then provide them with a wholesome meal. Vines will twist and turn around tree trunks to seek sunlight.

Such consciousness helps living things overcome obstacles or dilemmas so they can be successful problem-solvers. Rather than waste time agonizing over why the problem even had to happen or what caused it, the point in nature has always been to solve the problem simply. Because nature's living things are devoid of pride and free from the constraints of rigidity, it's easier for them to adjust to the changes and challenges presented by problems and to find the best way to overcome them.

How do you solve the problems in your life? Do you use a positive, tough-minded approach? Do you face a problem with anger — seeking whomever or whatever is responsible — or with trepidation — doubting your ability to effectively solve the problem or find the "right" solution?

If, while walking in the woods on day, you tripped over a dead log on the path, fell, and skinned your knee, you could hobble home, clean the wound, and tape a bandage over it. But if, on the next day, you tripped over the same dead log on the path, what would you do? You could treat your injury again and again, but it's never going to get better, and you're never going to enjoy your walk, until you solve the whole problem once and for all.

The best kind of problem-solving is the one that nature teaches us — that by being curious, by employing what you know, and by being unafraid of what you don't know, you just may find a good solution. The other ravens that were in the cage with the suspended food eventually began to pull up on the string too, but none mimicked the exact actions of the first raven. That means that each raven, while they may have been inspired by watching the first raven, applied its own skill, knowledge, and "style" to obtain the food. One raven moved sideways along the pole during successive stages of holding the string with its food; two others piled the string in loops.

There was one more raven, however; this last raven never did obtain the suspended food. But perhaps this raven was more human, and therefore spent more time wondering why its handlers had stopped their former feeding methods to adopt a new, more difficult one!

Stability

*"Monotony is the law of nature.
Look at the monotonous manner
in which the sun rises."*

— Mahatma Gandhi

There may be many different words and phrases you use to describe your view of stability, such as rigidity, routine, inflexibility, tedium, same-old same-old, ho-hum, and monotonous. Stability, to you, may be symbolized by all those routines you have to go through each day that may, at times, become so tedious and so annoying that you want to cry out, "I'm so tired of this!"

While craving variation, longing for a change of pace, needing to break out of the routine, and striving to be more spontaneous and flexible are certainly healthy desires, some things in your life need to stay the same. Knowing how to balance this need for a certain level of

stability in your life with the need to break out of a routine from time to time can be confusing.

At times you may enjoy the sense of expectation, dependability, security, and familiarity that comes as a result of a nondisrupted daily schedule, from a usual way of doing things, and from the sure-things on which you can depend. Nature has such a dependable routine, as described in *The Gospel According to Zen*:

*"Day after day the sun rises in the east;
Day after day the sun sets in the west."*

Nature, too, has the consistency of the four seasons, migrations and returns, new growths and harvests, constant renewal and eventual death, endless evolutions, eternal cycles. Everything in nature acts in conformity with a stable natural law that ensures the constancy of birth, life, and death.

Other times, however, you may long to interrupt the usual progression of your time and do something out of the ordinary. Nature, too, has such a need to break out of routine, with unpredictable winds and storms, lighting and thunder, droughts and floods. Even nature's rain can be different each time, as described by English poet and nature writer Edward Thomas: "... the early momentous thunderdrops, the perpendicular cataract shining, or at night the little showers, the spongy mists, the tempestuous mountain rain."

In many ways, instability becomes stability. There has to be an overall framework for things in the universe — which there is — but within that framework, there can be many random happenstances that make for differences and variations within the entire system. One of nature's most stable forces is that of gravity, for example, but gravity doesn't necessarily ensure stability; one loose rock on a mountainside can result in a great deal of instability when a rockslide results from gravity's pull on the loose rock.

Nature teaches you that you must have some sort of order to start from; that is, somewhere in your life, there must be some level of stability. So you can choose to live your life as a vagabond, a hobo, or a beach bum, but within that life there needs to be some semblance of structure and stability — a shelter you return to at night, for instance, a friend upon whom you can depend for a hot meal or good conversation, a favorite place to visit or a rock that feels good when you sit on it, a dog for your traveling companion. Likewise, you can choose to live your life in a very structured, disciplined way — as a member of a religious order or military force or by fulfilling the role that requires following a certain way of doing things — but you also need opportunities to suspend discipline and ignore the structures from time to time.

In the universe, there will always be certainty and uncertainty. How you balance the two in your life will determine if you'll live a monotonous, unfulfilling life; a life that's filled with noise, hustle-and-bustle, confusion, and chaos; or a life that provides you with a safe, secure foundation — a foundation that would be like, according to writer Susan St. John Rheault, "Granite. Of purpose. Of endeavor. Our efforts. Upon which we build." Such a foundation represents a stability that'll always be there — even when you choose to leave it from time to time.

Nonresistance

"Rapids are a challenge. Dangerous though they may be, no one who has known the canoe trails of the north does not love their thunder and the rush of them. No man who has portaged around white water, studied the swirls, the smooth, slick sweeps, and the V's that point the way above the breaks, has not wondered if he should try. Is there any suspense that quite compares with that moment of commitment when the canoe then is taken by its unseen power? Rapids can be run in larger craft, but it is in a canoe that one really feels the power of it."

— naturalist Sigurd F. Olson

In order to teach new pilots how to avoid panic and stress in emergency flight situations, flight instructors usually spend hours drilling students on everything from preflight inspections — to ensure that the airplane has been adequately and accurately inspected before take-off — to being on a vigilant lookout, while in-flight, for a field, pasture, or other safe sight on which to land in case the pilot needs to make a forced landing.

But all the knowledge and foresight in the world often can't give the student the appropriate preparation in knowing how to instinctively respond in an emergency situation. That's why many flight instruc-tors, during routine flight instruction, will suddenly force the airplane into an emergency situation, such as by pulling back on the throttle and drastically cutting power, and ask the student, "Well? What are you going to do now?" Students then have to show that they can handle the emergency situation; they must do this long before they learn how to fly solo. For it's not enough for them to be able to anticipate emergencies and know what ought to be done; rather, it's vital that they know what actions need to be taken and then to be able to take them without hesitation and without being overwhelmed by panic, fear, or doubt. Responding to in-flight emergencies, rather than reacting to them, allows a new, more peaceful pattern to emerge in the midst of a crisis — a pattern of nonresistance.

Nonresistance helps shift a negative situation to a positive one. Practicing nonresistance allows you to transcend hostility, fear, anger, guilt, overreaction, and other ineffective responses so you can take charge, identify whatever problem needs to be resolved, dispel any fears or doubts that may hinder your ability to reach a positive solution, and do whatever you need to do in any given situation. Being nonresistant means that you can let go of a desired outcome, shift your focus away from an end result, and simply take the necessary action; right action will then automatically right the situation.

Nonresistance in nature is epitomized by a mighty river. Except for occasional flooding, the river will flow within its banks. It will flow where it finds openings between cliffs and rocks. If the river is dammed, if the cliff is removed, or if the boulders are shifted, the river will simply flow a different course. The direction the river flows can be affected through change, but the river will still flow.

So, too, can it be in your life. If you move to another city, life will certainly change for you. If you take another job, things will invariably be different for you. If you marry, get divorced, or become widowed, your life will be radically altered. Whatever changes you actively choose to make in your life or must make due to circumstances that are forced upon you, whether such changes are big or small, will affect how your life flows. If you resist such changes — for example, if you long to return to the way things were and therefore struggle to cling to the past — then you'll never be able to flow with the ease of nonresistance.

Life is a flow of energy; it keeps the rivers flowing, your heart beating, the tides going in and out, and the clouds floating high in the sky. Nonresistance safeguards this flow. Learn from nature's nonresistance by listening to your intuition, drawing from your knowledge and wisdom, and taking action when you're in a calm, clear space. Always operate from a neutral position — one that strives to be unaffected by change and negativity — so that when your vision is clear, you'll be able to act successfully in situations in ways that maintain peace and harmony within yourself and with the world around you.

Relationships

*"You can grow intimate with almost any living thing,
transfer to it your own emotion of tenderness, nostalgia, regret, so that
often of a relationship one remembers the scene with the most affection.
A particular line of hedge in a Midland county, a drift of leaves in
a particular wood: it is only human to imagine that we receive back
from these the feeling someone left with them."*

— English writer Graham Greene

Long long ago, there was a young member of a king's court who was sent a great distance into the countryside to deliver a message from the king to the villagers in one of the kingdom's far territories. The king's messenger rode for several days, then paused at a stream just outside the village to let his thirsty horse drink. As he stretched his weary limbs, he heard the melodious sounds of a lute coming from somewhere nearby. He listened for a short time but then, because he was a passionate musician himself, he dismounted from his horse, reached into his saddlebags, and pulled out his own lute. Whereupon he began to play as he stepped in the direction of the sound of the other lute. Soon he came across a young goatherd who was sitting down near the stream, playing as he watered his herd.

Now in those days it was unheard of for a member of the king's court to associate with any commoner. But the two men continued to play together for several minutes; their playing was as smooth and yet as lively as the sparkling stream that flowed by them. When they stopped playing, they chatted for awhile, and soon a friendship was forged. As they parted they agreed to meet at the same spot along the stream on the same day each year to renew their love of music.

115

Many years went by, with the two men from different classes of life honoring their commitment to meet once a year at the same location. They continued to play their lutes together and talk for hours. Although each man confessed that they had, where they lived, other music lovers with whom they could play their lutes and share their passion for music, each vowed that they were "true comrades."

As the years marched on, the commoner began to look thin and pale; his clothes appeared ragged and his sandals quite worn. Often his now-wealthy and important friend would offer him money, a position on king's court, or many other amenities that would ease the man's poverty, but the man politely refused. "My friend, what drew us together was not the desire for gold," the man replied. "What we have sought together as friends is the riches that come from playing our music together, to the accompaniment of the orchestra that nature provides for us. That is what makes our friendship so very special."

Several more years passed, with each man never failing to appear at the mountain stream, lute in hand, each year. Then one year, the wealthy, gray-haired man showed up at the appointed spot on the special day to share music with his long-time companion. But his friend wasn't there. He waited for hours; the shadows grew around him, and night soon fell. He tried to play alone, but the sound that emanated from his lute sounded lonely and forlorn.

Sadly, he packed his lute in his saddle bags, then rode into the nearby village to inquire about his friend. There, he was informed that his friend had died within the past year. The man fought back tears as he mounted his horse and rode back to the spot by the stream where he had first met his friend. In sorrow, he broke his lute and tossed it in the stream. "With my true friend gone from the world," he wailed, "who will I play my music for?"

Yet each year until he died the king's messenger continued to come to the same spot where he and his friend once made beautiful music together. Rather than play, he would lie on the soft grass, close his eyes, and listen to the sounds that nature played for him — the stream, the wind, the trees, the grass, the birds. All reminded him of the true, rare harmony he had shared for so many years with his blessed friend.

Giving and Receiving

"All animals rightly distrust human beings; but when they once feel sure that they do not mean to hurt them, their confidence becomes so great that a man must be worse than a barbarian to abuse it."

— Swiss-born French philosopher Jean-Jacques Rousseau

For centuries bottlenose dolphins have treated humans with tolerance and even trust. Stories abound of their rescues of drowning swimmers, the excitement they exhibit in swimming next to boats on the open sea, their cooperative spirit in driving schools of fish into anglers' nets, their ability to mimic sounds as well as in the "dolphinese" language they use to communicate, and their affinity for touch that has led some trainers in zoos to use pats on the snout instead of food as rewards. There's even a beach in western Australia where a community of dolphins regularly strands itself for the pleasure of humans, sometimes even ignoring the fish being tossed to them and bringing instead their own gifts of fish and seaweed for the humans who stand on shore to greet them.

How have humans responded to the dolphins' giving nature? Some scientists have downplayed the actions of the charming sea creatures, stating that what appears to be the dolphins reaching out to humans is, in reality, natural dolphin behavior that really has nothing to do with humans. So when dolphins swim next to boats, for example, scientists say the dolphins are merely enjoying a free, speedy ride on a bow wave. When dolphins lift drowning humans to the surface, they're only doing so because of their instinctive tendencies to buoy up the bodies of ailing dolphins. And when dolphins guide fish into nets to be caught, they're only using their natural "fish-herding" abilities.

Yet no matter what the explanation is for their behaviors, dolphins clearly seem to be more attracted to humans than afraid of them. And, in the highly evolved animal society they've created, which appears to be based on a giving and receiving spirit, the dolphins seem to welcome humans into their "fold." Drowning swimmers who have been lifted to safety by the dolphins report that their rescues are gentle, efficient, and oftentimes persistent in the effort exerted to ensure a safe rescue. Perhaps the dolphins are merely treating the swimmers as they would any dolphin that's sick or injured rather than giving to the swimmer in the sense that humans equate with giving. But studies done of dolphin group rescues reveal that dolphins will immediately respond to a sick or injured dolphin's distress signal, locate the "victim," and then lift an ailing dolphin for each breath it needs to take day after day. Then, as the dolphin heals, they'll continue to provide intermittent support for weeks thereafter. Such selfless caretaking has its parallel in the human world, with caregivers who willingly devote time and energy to ailing loved ones.

How have humans received the giving of the dolphins? Off the Japanese island of Iki, thousands of dolphins are slaughtered every year by fisherman who are doing so in order to protect their own fishing grounds from such "competitors." In other parts of the world, dolphins are routinely killed for human consumption or used for bait. In the United States, dolphins have been trained and then used to retrieve mines that are too dangerous for human divers; many dolphins have lost their lives doing so. And, for years, because tuna and dolphins normally swim together, the tuna industry routinely captured dolphins in nets; most drowned before fishing crews could release them, while other crews didn't even attempt releases. Today a number of United States tuna companies have a "dolphin-safe" label on their cans of tuna, but dolphins are still dying horrible deaths in fishing nets around the world.

All living things participate in the process of giving and receiving, yet humans are the only living creatures that seek to receive and then carefully dole out how much is given in return. It has only been in the past few decades that humankind has begun to realize the error of its ways — in the depletion of valuable natural resources, of taking without replenishing, about effectively eradicating vital species from the planet.

English statesman and writer Thomas More has written, "To take something from yourself, to give to another, that is humane and gentle and never takes away as much comfort as it brings again." Learn to live by these words and, as well, learn to appreciate the delicate balance of giving and receiving that nature so willingly offers humankind. As Jacques-Yves Cousteau once commented, "It means nothing to strike up a friendship with a sea lion or a dolphin if, at the same time, we are destroying their last refuges along our coasts and our islands. It is an exercise in vanity and absurdity to try to communicate with a killer whale and then to put it on exhibition in an aquatic zoo as a circus freak." Treat all of nature's living things as you would want to be treated. Give and receive with love and compassion.

Control

"Let us a little permit Nature to take her own way;
she better understands her own affairs than we."

— French essayist Michel Eyquem de Montaigne

Life depends upon the integrity of the entire biological world. All species fit together in an intricate, interdependent, self-sustaining whole, like pieces in a jigsaw puzzle. Even one missing piece out of a thousand interlocking pieces will make the puzzle incomplete; each piece is necessary for the picture to be complete.

One single action, which may impact on only one single species, can actually affect the future of the planet's entire ecosystem. Deforestation in Central America, for example, does more than just destroy trees and strip away valuable topsoil. The North American summer insects, which winter in those forests, are also destroyed, and without the insects, the population of North American songbirds, which needs the insects for their diet, declines. One single act of paving a meadow ends up depriving thousands of honeybees from the food they need to produce the honey that can help them to survive through a winter. The production of one single edition run of a large-city Sunday newspaper can destroy nearly seventy-five thousand trees. All this has led Biologist Paul Ehrlich to estimate that human beings usurp, either directly or indirectly, about forty percent of each year's total biological production. Thus, in effect, there's really nothing that humankind is *not* degrading.

The essential biodiversity that you need in order to live can't be protected by letter-writing campaigns, '60s-style sit-ins to halt production, a check that's written to a nonprofit organization which — although nobly written — often goes into the hands of administrators rather than those living things that should be administered to, or by sending a few favored species — before they die out — to live out their days in a zoo. As American zoo director Jack Hanna has pointed out, "We may be able to survive in a world where the giant panda, the California condor and the black rhino exist only as pictures in a book. But do we want to?"

Throughout the years nature has taught humankind that, when left alone, living things can maintain themselves without zookeepers, park rangers, foresters, plans, schemes, and all sorts of other representations of human interference. That's because nature knows how to exert natural control over its populations. Nature has always had control over its own system in order to ensure the reproduction and survival of each living thing, but humankind refuses to respect such control. There's hardly a place on Earth where people don't log, hunt, pave, spray, drain, divert, graze, plow, mine, strip, burn, drill, spill, or dump. All this has led writer, farmer, broadcaster, and former state legislator Will Curtis to comment, "To maintain our planet and our lives, [all] the other species have similar requests, all of which add up to: Control yourselves. Control your numbers. Control your greed. See yourselves as who you are, part of an interdependent biological community, the most intelligent part, though you don't often act that way. *Act that way*. Do so either out of a moral respect for something wonderful that you did not create and do not understand, or out of a practical interest in your own survival."

Just one generation ago, most people bought food in bulk at local stores. You probably remember being in the kitchen of your mother or grandmother and seeing, on the counter top, canisters filled with sugar, tea, rice, flour, coffee, and other dry goods that were purchased in reusable cotton bags. But you live in a "paper or plastic" world today; there are very few items you purchase that aren't wrapped in plastic, packed in plastic, or bagged in plastic.

Can you learn to have such control in your life — to learn how not to waste things in your own home and business? Can you start to have an impact on controlling the amount of new construction that's being done your neighborhood or the city or town in which you live by showing your opposition to the continued destruction of natural areas? Can you visit museums, local zoos, and nearby aquariums and observe the treatment of the animals that are being held in captivity to ensure that there's no abuse? Can you purchase less plastic and less packaged materials and buy in larger quantities or in bulk? Can you exert more control in your life by becoming aware of how much you crave and by starting to limit such excesses?

Can you do all these things — and more? Your fate depends upon it.

Heritage

"But if adventure has a final and all-embracing motive it is surely this: we go out because it is in our nature to go out, to climb the mountains and sail the seas, to fly to the planets and plunge into the depths of the oceans. By doing these things we make touch with something outside or behind, which strangely seems to approve our doing them. We extend our horizon, we expand our being, we revel in a mastery of ourselves..."

— writer Wilfred Noyce

Do you have faith in yourself that, if you had to, you could survive "out in the wild" for a period of time? In 1957 Lieutenant David Steeves hiked out of California's rugged Sierra Mountains fifty-four days after reports that he and his Air Force trainer jet had disappeared; he lived in the rugged wilderness for nearly two months after parachuting from his disabled plane. There have certainly been many other incredible stories you've read about human survival in the wild — people have clung to buoys in stormy seas for several hours after their boat has capsized, others have survived plane crashes in remote areas and lived for long periods of time

prior to being rescued, hikers have become lost and disoriented in the woods and ended up being found safe and sound days — and sub-zero temperatures and blizzards — later.

Sometimes people have purposely placed themselves in dangerous survival situations by scaling mountains, diving deep into oceans, crossing deserts, voyaging to remote islands, and rocketing into outer space. Pole expedition leader Sir Ernest Shackleton quickly formed the group that accompanied him by calling for members to join his tortuous foray into the frigid elements with the following notice: "Men wanted for hazardous journey, small wages, bitter cold, long months of complete darkness — constant danger, safe return doubtful — honor and recognition in case of success."

For years humankind has endured and survived incredible things; for years humankind has accepted dangerous missions and outings involving great risks that have not only tested but often pushed the limits of human endurance. Do you trust that you could survive as well as others have if you were thrust into a similar situation to theirs, where you would be called upon to test your limits, your strength, your endurance, your knowledge, and your courage in being able to handle the challenges of the wilderness?

People go out into the wilderness in a variety of ways — hiking, boating, camping, whitewater rafting, mountain climbing, hiking, and canoeing — because they want to. They go out for the fun of it, the pleasure of it, the challenge of it, the stress-relieving elements of it, and the shared companionship of it. As well, they go out to learn more about the natural world and its living things. But they also go out because they have to — because they feel the pull of nature's heritage deep within

them. "There are circuits and juices in every person," explains writer Douglas H. Chadwick, "that are the heritage of millions of years of evolution and survival in wild country. They need exercising. Add a twinge of fear and wonder, and they can bring the world into focus with astonishing clarity. In such a setting, far from the clutter and clang of modern life, you find your senses opening wide, flowing easily, like the river, touching everything.... And you realize...why had we come, if not to be dependent upon our own resources and, in so doing, discover more about them?"

The heritage that nature brings to all living things is not the battle against the elements or the battle against rivals and enemies, but the battle against oneself. In order to learn how to be independent in this world — both the natural world and the man-made — you need to learn how to be dependent upon yourself. You need to learn how to be dependent upon your own resources, upon your own capabilities, upon your own intelligence, upon your own instincts and gut responses, upon your own beliefs, upon your own strengths.

Nature shows you that you have a place in the living heritage of life every time you look around you at the passion, the challenges, the grandeur, the beauty, the discipline, and the opportunities represented by all of nature's wonders. Each and every wonder is a part of you; you are as profound as the sea, as gentle as a summer breeze, as beautiful as the side of a mountain, as soft as the warm sand, as active as the environment in which you live.

Your heritage encourages you to be strong. Your heritage helps you to trust and have faith in yourself. Your heritage implores you to act. Your heritage urges you to sometimes abandon the search for security and reach out to the risk of living. Your heritage tells you to accept living and dying equally. Your heritage stretches your mind and body. Your heritage pushes you to go out often, to go out into the Great Unknown in order to know more about yourself and the world around you.

Communication

"'Why, one can hear and see the grass growing!'
thought Levin, noticing a wet, slate-colored aspen leaf
moving beside a blade of young grass."

— Russian writer Leo Tolstoy

Because you can't communicate directly from mind to mind with others, you may often find that communication misinterpretations are a frequent problem. What you say and what you mean are often not in synch. As well, the words you say can often be interpreted in many ways or have double meanings. Hand motions and gestures you use may be misconstrued. Eye contact you make with another can be interpreted as attentiveness, a warning, or a sexual invitation. The written word can sometimes be misleading or fail to express what you really want to say.

Communication between human beings can oftentimes be so confusing and individualized that even a dozen witnesses to the same event can't agree on a single account; each sees and hears something different, based on his or her own interpretation. What this means is that human communication is relative and subjective; there are no absolute truths, and there always seem to be varying degrees of ambiguity in what is said and what is heard.

Yet in the natural world there's no room for such ambiguity or unclarity; clear communication is so essential can it mean the difference between life and death. Take, for example, the alarm vocalizations used by the vervet monkeys, which live in the forests and open

areas of Africa. Since the monkeys are about the size of a small dog, they're vulnerable to attack by three different predators. Evading each predator requires its own specific response. Vervet monkeys communicate which predator is a current threat by using one of three distinct alarm calls. The differentiation of alarm calls is critical, for the type of alarm call indicates the type of danger, which then indicates the correct, life-saving response. The response to a leopard call, for instance, is to climb into a tree. But since the leopards are good climbers, the monkeys escape from them by climbing out onto the smallest branches. Yet this makes them vulnerable to an attack from the martial eagle, another predator; the correct response to an alarm call for the eagle is for the monkeys to move into thick vegetation close to a tree trunk or at ground level —where they wouldn't be safe from the leopard. In response to the snake alarm call, the monkeys simply stand on their hind legs and look around on the ground, which leaves them vulnerable to an attack from a leopard as well as an eagle.

Thus, since the best ways to escape from the three principal predators are mutually exclusive, it's important that the alarm calls inform other members of the group which danger threatens them. A generalized alarm call and escape plan would not only be inefficient — climbing into a tree to avoid a snake would be a waste of time and effort — but may also be costly, for mistaking an eagle for a leopard or vice versa could easily put the monkeys' lives in danger. Thus, when the monkeys hear the leopard alarm call what's being clearly communicated to them is "Go climb a tree." When they hear the snake alarm call they know to immediately stand up and look around. One call, one response; another call, a different response. The monkeys communicate with one another clearly.

This is just one example of how nature's living things are superb communicators with one another. Yet nature also communicates clearly with you, if you take the time to listen. The sound the rain makes on your roof communicates to you the type of rain it is — a gentle sprinkle, a steady rain, or a downpour. Rustling in the leaves communicates the presence of a living creature moving about on the ground. The surge of waves against the shore communicates a calm or stormy sea. The first warble of a bird communicates daybreak. The hoot of an owl signals that night has fallen and the hunt is on. The whine of a mosquito near your ear warns of a tiny prick.

Nature teaches you to accept that words will always be imperfect. The gestures and tones used by human beings don't always coincide with the thoughts, feelings, requests, or needs that are being expressed. But nature communicates to you in ways which, though subtle, are distinct and clear. All you need to do is look, be silent, and listen. As Irish writer James Joyce has interpreted the ocean's communication with man, "Listen: a fourworded wavespeech: seesoo, hrss, rsseeiss, ooos. Vehement breath of waters amid seasnakes, rearing horses, rocks. In cups of rocks it slops: flop, slop, slap: bounded in barrels. And, spent, its speech ceases. It flows purling, wisely flowing, floating foampool, flower unfurling."

Take time to pay attention nature's communication with you. You'll find it a lovely conversation!

Deception

*"Look at a tiger. The light and dark of his stripes
and the black edge encircling the white patch on his ear help him
to look like the jungle with flecks of sun on it."*

— American poet Marianne Moore

Camouflage hunting clothes can be quite effective in hiding from the animal being hunted; rather than look like a person, the outfit enables you to blend in with a pile of leaves, tree trunks, or the reeds by the edge of lake. The appearance you create by using such camouflage is illusory and false and yet, it's also real.

Animals have used camouflage for centuries, sometimes to keep from being eaten, and sometimes to get what they want to eat to move close enough so it can be caught. The American bittern's long, striped neck seems to disappear when the bird is standing still in the cattails and grasses in which it lives. Sometimes the bird will even sway with the grasses in a breeze, further camoflaging itself both from its predators and the fish it preys upon. The ground-nesting American woodcock blends with the dead leaves in which it incubates its eggs; later, the hatchlings themselves are concealed by their color. The spotted coat on the white-tailed deer fawn helps hide the creature from predators in the sun-dappled woodlands where it lives. And countershading — or the differences in color between an animal's belly and its back — create an important blending protection as well. For example, when bright sunlight reflects off the dark back feathers of the lesser yellowlegs, it casts a shadow on their light-colored breasts, enabling the birds to "melt" into their habitat.

Deception is one of the lessons humankind has learned well from nature. "Keeping up appearances" is a goal quite often effectively employed in the business world and with family members, an intimate partner, friends, and even enemies; it allows you to create an effect for others that may not necessarily be true, and lets you use this effect to hide from them. This can help you to slyly step behind an illusion you've created so you don't have to let others "see" who you really are. If you employ the tactics of the greatest natural deceiver of all — the chameleon — you can be seen as the person others want you to be or even who you want to be. Like an actor or actress who's playing a role, you can create a false character in order to keep your "true" character from being exposed.

Yet deception can be one of nature's most misunderstood lessons. For nature doesn't use deception to lie, cheat, manipulate, to avoid intimacy, or to be dishonest in any way; rather, nature uses deception for survival. So why, then, would you want to deceive others through the appearances you create? Sometimes it's because you're too afraid to let others see the true you; sometimes it's because

you don't even know who the true you is.

In many Eastern countries, people believe that truth is found after scaling a high mountain peak and consulting a wise sage. That's almost what you need to do to find your truth. You need to set off on a challenging journey that will bring you into a closer consultation with your inner self as well as with the natural world around you. Yet you don't have to reach the top of some majestic peak, walk the Appalachian Trail, or run a marathon in order to find this truth. Rather, you can realize the truth along the way of life's challenging journey. As you use the knowledge about all the truths you discover about the world and about yourself, your journey through life can become easier and less filled with deceptions and camouflages.

Your search for truth is an on-going quest; as well, it's a quest that has to avoid camouflages and deceptions in order to be meaningful. Sometimes this means that you'll be more susceptible to hurt and pain inflicted from those who thrive on deception. But, over time, you'll become stronger. As Robert Frost once wrote, "Something we were withholding made us weak until we found out that it was ourselves we were withholding from the land of the living."

Fragility

"What is life: It is the flash of a firefly in the night.
It is the breath of a buffalo in the winter time; it is the little shadow
which runs across the grass and loses itself in the sunset."

— Crowfoot Indian

On a dark and rainy night some time soon in a location near you, when the temperature is about forty-five degrees and it may be hard for you to negotiate driving because of a low-lying fog, scores of salamanders and wood frogs and other amphibious creatures will crawl out from their burrows in upland woodlands and, using their mysterious reptilian navigation systems, will make their way to the vernal pools where they themselves were spawned. Some of the creatures will reach the pools and achieve their goal: to breed, deposit fertile eggs, and return to the woods. Some, because they live as long as twenty years, will be making yet another journey

like the others they've made before. But many will die along the way, crushed under the wheels of passing cars.

In just one instant every year in the spring, a large portion of a future population of a single species is eradicated during its mating migration. One herpetologist who has kept statistics on amphibian migrations across one site of the same stretch of road in Lexington, Massachusetts since the 1960s noted that, over the years, the salamander road-kill rate had risen to as high as fifty percent. Where she used to see hundreds of salamanders at that site during migration time, the numbers steadily declined over the years. This led her to take her

findings on the yellow spotted salamander's mortality rate to the town's conservation administrator. With town approval, they have been able to close two roads to through traffic for two salamander-friendly nights each year.

During one spring salamander crossing night in Lexington, one of the volunteers manned a roadblock, explaining to motorists the reason for the closing. Rather than be annoyed or upset, many motorists simply parked their cars and joined the nearly one hundred volunteers who were safeguarding the lives of the salamanders. Flashlights were handed out; people walked along the road, alert for the creatures. "A lot of neighbors come with children," one volunteer explained. "Kids love it. It's pitch dark, but they have very good eyes. They pick the salamanders up and carry them across until about ten o'clock."

Yet providing such life-saving assistance for a creature as simple as a salamander isn't unusual. In Germany, for instance, salamander protection systems abound. Along roads, at many of the favorite salamander crossing sites, traffic signs and flashing lights have been installed. In some places fences have been erected to herd the salamanders into an underground tunnel that then leads them safely under the road to their spawning pools.

What good do such actions do? By protecting the salamander, humankind is also helping to keep the insect population under control. Male salamanders that reach the vernal pools are able to successfully deposit spermatophores in the water, which the female salamanders later take into their bodies. The females then lay egg masses that look like clear jelly on the pond's surface. The babies hatch about six weeks later and then spend the next three to four months in the pond in a larval stage. At this time in their growth they're quite predaceous, feeding voraciously on aquatic insects until they're mature enough to leave the pool and find their own upland holes to live in. So without the larva, the aquatic insects would have no predator.

But why go to such great lengths to ensure the salamanders' safety by closing roads and asking people to seek alternate routes? For many reasons. Because nature teaches that humankind is always part of the future — a future that only humans possess a power to shape in a negative way as well as a positive one. Because nature teaches that all living things are bound too tightly together to let any one be spared. Because nature teaches that in order for life to be sustained, the ten thousand links in nature's chain must forever be joined and never be broken. And because, as American entomologist Edward O. Wilson once remarked, "When you have seen one ant, one bird, one tree, you have not seen them all."

Movement

"I was born by the sea and I have noticed that all the great events in my life have taken place by the sea. My first idea of movement, of the dance, certainly came from the rhythms of the waves."

— American dancer Isadora Duncan

Nature teaches you that the only universal meaning to life that holds true for everyone is that no living thing is ever going to get out of it alive. So rather than waste time and energy trying to understand why you're here, where you're going, or why you have to face some of the trials you do, nature suggests that perhaps the best approach to life is to simply move with it for as long as you can.

Life is meant to be lived in motion, for all living things are in motion. Deep below the ocean's surface, for example, aquatic plant life undulates in the currents. Corals, which are actually made up of colonies of thousands of tiny animals that live in separate, chalky tubes, are rarely still. Each animal, called a polyp, feeds by waving its stinging tentacles from its tube to catch baby fish and other tiny sea animals. Coral colonies grow to make rocky coral islands; rings of chalky rock that form around the island are called coral reefs. Coral reefs are built in warm, shallow seas, where the constantly moving water brings fresh food "deliveries" to coral animals such as sea sponges, anemones, sea urchins, starfish, and many kinds of sea worms.

The constant motion also extends outward from the reef, for several kinds of fish live in or near the reef. Small fish flit quickly back and forth, feeding on microscopic animal and plant life, called plankton. Larger fish propel themselves around, oftentimes feeding on the smaller fish. Sharks and barracuda, octopus, moray eels, trunkfish, surgeonfish, butterfly fish, and triggerfish all move about in their own particular "transportation styles" around the corals and sea fans. For example, the monkfish — or angler — which lies on the bottom, waves a "wand" over its great mouth to attract smaller fish. Other fish that live near the surface of the water or in shallow seas oftentimes live in schools that move about as if all the school members had rehearsed their synchronized patterns for years — anchovies, pilotfish, bluefin tuna, dolphinfish, and the ocean bonito, or tuna.

Along the coastline, in rock pools and shallows, lobsters and crabs crawl about while waves splash against the shore. Overhead gulls, terns, gannets, and other sea birds scan the shallow waters for something to eat, while shore birds like the sea campion and the oystercatcher "power walk" back and forth along the sandy stretches of beach, taking breaks to thrust their beaks like rapiers into the sand for tasty treats. Periwinkles, whelks, mussels, and starfish lazily soak in warm tidal pools.

The shores and sea cliffs are also in living motion; they're particularly busy places in the spring, aswarm with nesting birds. Cliff tops and rocky islands provide nesting sites for puffins, gulls, and gannets. Ledges are filled with razorbills, murres, and kittiwakes. Cormorants and shags nest on the rocks close to the sea. Gray seals often flip-flop ashore to give birth in the spring.

All this represents only a small segment of nature's bountiful, bounding activities. Yet there's even more motion that can be glimpsed around the ocean — human motion. Watch those who daily prepare to cast off for their "office" at sea, and you'll find that observing a working harbor is like observing a colony of ants. From the unloading of fish to washing down decks to loading cargo, as well as the endless comings and goings of a number of sea-faring vessels — working boats, ocean-going ferries, cargo ships, deep-sea fishing boats, pleasure craft, lobster boats, and clamming rowboats — it's an exhausting, choreographed dance of life by the sea.

Nature, like life, ought never to be still. As William Shedd once said, "A ship in harbour is safe, but that is not what ships are built for." Participate in the dance of life that's forever going on around you. Climb, swim, fish, fly, buzz, jump, hop, dig, sing, twirl, swirl, dive — do all you can! Keep pace with the hustle and bustle of the natural world, and life will forever be a glorious, active adventure.

Controversy

"Once birds sang and flirted among the leaves while men, more helpless and less accomplished, skulked between the trunks below them. Now they linger in the few trees that men have left standing, or fit themselves into the chinks of the human world, into its church towers, lamp-posts, and gutters."

— English archaeologist and writer Jacquetta Hawkes

Few things express the controversy that surrounds nature as well as the opposing car bumper stickers "Save the Whales" and "Nuke the Whales." Humankind often becomes a population divided over what to do with nature. While few would deny nature's profound importance and impact in their lives, how such importance is regarded from one person to the next is often in diametric opposition. Where one person may look at a towering tree and see it as a beautiful part of the landscape, another looks at the tree and sees it as a source of raw materials for the construction of a beautiful piece of furniture. Where one person may marvel at the chance sighting of a deer or moose while walking through the woods, another may marvel at the sighting of the same woodland creature through a rifle scope. Where one person may be awed by the power of a great creature like an elephant or a rhinoceros, another may be awed by the money that can be earned by illegal poaching to obtain an elephant's ivory tusks and a rhinoceros's horns. Where one person may touch the coat of a mink or a fox and thrill at its soft texture, another may pay top dollar to thrill at the soft texture of a mink coat or a fox wrap. Where one person may become excited at the sighting of a coyote near a suburban area, another may incite armed citizens to kill the wild beast.

When the first Europeans came to North America, the continent was rich in natural resources — rich beyond anyone's wildest dreams. The primeval forests were alive with the sounds of nature, clear streams were well-stocked with fish, the earth was filled with minerals, and abundant wildlife more than amply supported the frontiersman, the farmer, and the businessman. No one at the time would have ever doubted that such bounties wouldn't last. Yet today it may be quite difficult to ever imagine what this country was like just a few centuries ago. As well, it may be next to impossible to describe what the planet must have been like for a farmer or shepherd who was alive in 6,000 B.C.

And yet controversy has always surrounded humankind's relationship with and its treatment of nature. As early in American history as 1854 Chief Seattle's speech to the Commissioner of Indian Affairs for the Washington Territory scolded the white man about his disregard for the earth, criticizing him by saying, "One portion of land is the same to him as the next, for he is a stranger who comes in the night and takes from the land whatever he needs. The earth is not his brother,

but his enemy, and when he has conquered it, he moves on.... He treats his mother the earth and his brother the sky as things to be bought and plundered, sold like sheep or bright beads. His appetite will devour the earth and leave behind only a desert." Ten years after Chief Seattle's speech, Vermont lawyer and the man credited as America's first environmentalist — George Perkins Marsh — published a book called *Man and Nature: Physical Geography as Modified by Human Action*. In his book, Marsh anticipated the crisis in pollution, overpopulation, and vanishing resources and condemned man as being "no asset to the earth."

The controversy that surrounds nature today comes from recognition that the planet is more than just a home for humankind; it's a living biosphere that humankind no longer lives *on* but lives *in*. Every breath you take draws oxygen out of the air and replaces it with carbon dioxide; picnic under a tree, and you give the tree your unwanted carbon dioxide while the tree trades you its life-sustaining oxygen. Thus, both you and the tree need each other for your continued existence; as well, both you and nature need one another for the planet to survive. As John Steinbeck has written, "Can you live without a willow tree? Well, no, you can't. The willow tree is you."

You may see this point of view and respect it, or you may not; therein lies the controversy of how to best interact with nature. And yet nature teaches you not to shy away from such controversy. Because nature is all living things and one of those living things is you, in questioning the existence of any living thing you're also questioning your existence. So "What is its value?" is not the question you need to ask when one of nature's living things is being threatened. Rather, ask, "What is my value?" How you respond will provide you with an enlightening lesson and valuable insight into your regard for the worth of any living thing.

Mystery

"The great affair, the love affair with life, is to live as variously as possible, to groom one's curiosity like a high-spirited thoroughbred, climb aboard, and gallop over the thick, sun-struck hills every day. Where there is no risk, the emotional terrain is flat and unyielding, and, despite all its dimensions, valleys, pinnacles, and detours, life will seem to have none of its magnificent geography, only a length. It began in mystery, and it will end in mystery, but what a savage and beautiful country lies in between."

— American poet and writer Diane Ackerman

Do you realize how mysterious the natural world really is? Although you may study it endlessly, spend a great deal of time in it, and feel that you're truly "in touch" with it, in reality you, as a human being, are quite out of touch with the natural world. That's because compared to living things that are far less developed than you are, your ability to truly "be in touch" with the world around you is quite inferior. As well, you only have a limited awareness of what your senses do detect. Right now, for example, your body is being inundated with uncountable waves, forces, sounds, and particles to which your natural detectors

— your five senses — are blind. A compass needle is more sensitive to magnetic forces that you don't even feel. Your dog hears sounds that are well beyond your range of hearing. A seismograph registers movements in the earth crust that you aren't aware of. And neutrinos, incredibly tiny particles that originate from deep in the sun, zip through your body every second, day and night — about 100 million of them — with your being none the wiser!

Because your senses are attuned only to a limited amount of sensual activity that's going on around you, there's much you don't know about the world in which you live. An invisible world swirls all around you, totally undetected. Much, therefore, is unknown to you. Much is a mystery.

Most of the visible activity registered by your eyes, for example, is filtered out of your brain before it even reaches your consciousness. So your view of a marigold in the visible-light spectrum — the human spectrum — is far different from how flying insects would see the same flower, whose eyes are sensitive to ultraviolet light. A rattlesnake, on the other hand, "sees" in infrared light, which enables the hungry reptile to detect temperature differences as small as a quarter-degree Celsius up to over a foot away — meaning it can detect the warm body of nearby prey and thus be able to strike quickly to obtain its next meal.

Your sense of smell, too, is quite dull compared to other creatures. While you might think that wolves, coyotes, and other animals that depend upon hunting would have the keenest senses of smell, it's really the emperor moth that has far superior scenting abilities. Male moths can detect the sex attractor of a virgin female moth that's nearly seven miles away — upwind!

Touch, the most basic form of communication all living things have, has become so highly developed in fish that they can detect how fast they're moving through the help of an organ that's highly sensitive to the rate of water flowing past them. And, taste, which provides pleasure for humans, is vitally critical to the survival of other species. The salmon of the Pacific Northwest, for example, rely upon the subtle tastes and odors in the water in which they live to locate the specific river in which they were born so they can return to their birthplace to spawn. Even up to four years after leaving their river of birth, they unerringly find the river from which they came.

Hearing, the fifth sense, has been so highly refined in the Mexican free-tailed bat that in the Bracken Cave, near San Antonio, Texas, a mother can leave her offspring to hunt for food and then return to the cave population of twenty million bats and locate her single pup in order to feed it. She does this by emitting a high-pitched squeak that's inaudible to human ears, which bounces back as an echo from the cave walls and provides her with the specific region in the cave where she left her pup. She then hones in on squeaks from her own pup, ignoring the din from all the other mother-pup echolocation that's going on.

"Imagine," begins the opening lines of the movie *The Day of the Dolphin*, "that your life is spent in an environment of total physical sensation. That every one of your senses has been heightened to a level that in a human being might only be described as ecstatic. That you're able to see, to perceive, with every part of your being — sight, hearing, taste, smell — and that every inch of your surface, your skin, is a receptor, a continuous source of perfectly accurate information about the world for miles around."

If you were so sensitively developed, there'd probably be little you'd need to sense from the world around you. There'd probably be little you wouldn't understand about the natural world in which you live. There'd probably be no mystery to life.

But since you'll never be that highly developed, the natural world will always remain a mystery to you — one that can make for enjoyable learning with each new sensation you experience.

Unity

"A human being should be able to change a diaper, plan an invasion, butcher a hog, conn a ship, design a building, write a sonnet, balance accounts, build a wall, set a bone, comfort the dying, take orders, give orders, cooperate, act alone, pitch manure, solve equations, analyze a new problem, program a computer, cook a tasty meal, fight efficiently, die gallantly. Specialization is for insects."

— writer Robert A. Heinlein

Until the eighteenth century, people thought honey dropped from the sky and was then collected by bees. At least two of the world's greatest thinkers planted the seeds that led to that belief. Aristotle opined that "honey fell with the rising of the stars, and when the rainbow rests upon the earth." Pliny the Elder proposed that honey was "a saliva emanating from the stars, or a juice exuding from the air." Honey was thus harvested from the bees by breaking open the hives that the bees had constructed in trees, with little regard paid to maintaining the integrity of either the waxy honeycombs that were essential for the storage of honey

or the intricate society unity that was necessary for the hive to flourish.

Then, around 1500, clever harvesters constructed wooden hives that were built in layers so that the queen bee and her male drones could be kept separate from the busy female workers and the hustle-bustle of the production of honey in the honeycombs. Harvesters could then simply collect the honey from one layer without either destroying the waxy storage cells or disrupting the unity of the hive. But it was only after observant beekeepers determined that it was the bees themselves that actually produced the honey, in a processing plant type of operation, that attention

began to be paid to the unity of the hive and how each bee in a particular hive — which could consist of up to twenty thousand bees — provided an integral and specialized task at the honey-producing plant. Guard bees, it was observed, stayed at the entrance to the hive in order to "greet" the forager bees as they returned from the field and to make sure that the returning bees were members of the colony and not "enemy" bees that were on a "raid." Each of the foragers returned with one of three raw materials essential to sustaining life in the hive — pollen, which provides the bees with protein and is essential for raising their young; propolis, which is gathered from tree sap and is used as a kind of "hive superglue" to seal off and cover any cracks in the hive; and nectar, the source of all the honey, which is gathered from flowers, travels through the bee's esophagus into the honey sac, and is converted by enzymes the bee secretes into a mixture of glucose and fructose. When the forager bees returned to the hive, the house bees then began their specialized task of pumping water out of the nectar and assisting in the continuation of the chemical process that results in honey. Then, the hive as a whole worked together to fan the moisture out of the honey in order to reduce it to its finished state.

While some honeys are made from a primary source, no honey is made exclusively from just one source. Oftentimes bees must travel great distances on initial forays in order to locate a good source of pollen and nectar for the hive. When a single foraging worker has discovered a rich source of food, such as flowers that have just come into bloom, it returns to the hive and moves over the surface of the honeycomb in agitated patterns called dances that communicate to the other foragers its discovery. Within a matter of minutes, the foraging bees swarm to the location and begin their task of collection.

Bees are just one species of nature's living things that live in a highly specialized society, united by a common purpose and by performing tasks that are essential to that purpose. Specialization is critical for their unity; without it, they would die. You, however, live in a far different society, one that protects your rights to say, think, and act as you please; one that has essentially eliminated the rallying cry of "for the good of society" that would unify you and your fellow citizens for a common cause or purpose. Gone are the days that fostered the attitude of "we're all in this together" or the need to join with others to present a united front. You — and humankind — have moved far away from the principles upon which the American colonies — or "hives" — were originally founded. You are, in many ways, on your own.

While nature teaches you that human beings possess immense powers that ensure survival without the need for specialization, acting in unity with others is essential in helping you understand your special place in the universe, the contribution you can make to it, and the impact you can have — an impact that can be as significant as the one the bees have on the blossoms.

These things, in turn, increase your sensitivity to the harmony that's necessary to promote living unity in your world — a world that is made up of many intricate, specialized, and connected mini-societies in which the thousands of species thrive and survive. As beekeeper and writer Sue Hubbell explains, "Then there is that other appeal, the stronger one, of spending, during certain parts of the year, a ten- or twelve-hour working day with bees, which are, when all is said and done, simply a bunch of bugs. But spending my days in close and intimate contact with creatures who are structured so differently from humans, and who get on with life in such a different way, is like being a visitor in an alien but ineffably engaging world."

Individuality

"It is interesting to contemplate a tangled bank, clothed with many plants of different kinds, with birds singing on the bushes, with various insects flitting about, and with worms crawling through the damp earth, and to reflect that these elaborately constructed forms, so different from each other, and dependent upon each other in so complex a manner, have all been produced by laws acting around us."

— English naturalist and scientist Charles Darwin

What do you think it takes for you to feel like your own person, for you to believe yourself to be an individual? Some people think this means differentiating themselves as much as possible from others in a variety of ways — in their style of dress, the mannerisms they employ, the beliefs they develop. Some people think this means that by distinguishing themselves in situations that require uniformity — such as in the military or in the corporate world — they're perceived to be individuals. And still others strive to live by the philosophy proposed by Henry David Thoreau: "If a man does not keep pace with his companions, perhaps it is because he hears a different drummer. Let him step to the music he hears, however measured or far away."

Yet being more unique than others or marching to a different beat doesn't necessarily make you more of an individual. Ask a male toad why it's attracted to a particular female toad, and it will respond that it's attracted to "the two great round eyes coming out of her little head, her large flat mouth, her yellow belly, and brown back..."; in short, according to French writer and philosopher Voltaire, what the male toad is attracted to is the essential quality of "toadness" in the female. Yet within that sameness is a uniqueness —

an individuality — that enables the male toad to distinguish the female from hundreds of others in the same pond.

Nature teaches an important lesson in individuality through the nesting habits of birds. Long ago it was believed that all birds probably nested in the same way, laying their eggs in depressions on the ground or in natural cavities such as holes in trees. But, over time, bird nests became as varied and individualized as their occupants. Female Canada geese constructed nests of grasses to hold the eggs. Trumpeter swans formed nest mounds on ponds. Female mallards nested at the edge of ponds, lining the nest with their own down.

Other species decided they preferred to nest in holes. So woodpeckers chiseled nest cavities in rotting trees. Kingfishers and bank swallows dug burrows in river and stream banks and laid their eggs in the burrows. Tree swallows, bluebirds, and other cavity-nesters occupied old woodpecker holes.

Red-tailed hawks and goshawks opted for high-rise living. They used twigs and branches to build big platform nests in trees. Osprey and bald eagles built nests with very large sticks. The eagles built their homes in trees, but the ospreys decided to make use of man-made structures around them, such as power poles, duck blinds, and channel markers.

Female hummingbirds made tiny nest cups consisting of seed down, mosses, or lichen; they used cobwebs to bind their nests together. But the songbirds were by far the most individually creative birds of all; they made use of many kinds of materials to build a great variety of nests. Robins plastered their cup nests with mud and lined them with soft grasses. Orioles hung woven, pouch-like nests from branches. Great crested flycatchers incorporated shed snakeskins and pieces of cellophane into their nests.

To be an individual, you need to construct your own "nest." This nest can be an actual residence — an apartment or the home you've always dreamed of, decorated in the way you'd like it. Your nest can be constructed out of the tangible things in your life — possessions, people, or places you like to visit — that help you to feel as if you're your own person. Or your nest can be created from intangible things that provide you with a sense of your own identity — freedom from an addiction or dependency, time set aside for doing the things you'd like to do, the ability to express love to another.

Focus

"*The Trobrianders [natives who live in the Trobriand Islands off the northeast coast of Papua-New Guinea] are great voyagers because they know how to bide their time. They wait weeks for the weather to break, and then set sail; and if they feel a storm is coming on, they look for a rock or an atoll to find anchorage. If the weather is bad, they hunker down. It doesn't matter if a trip takes days or weeks; it is the same voyage. The idea is to see it through to the end.*"

— writer Paul Theroux

Have you ever tried to follow the flight of a hummingbird? It's not only the smallest bird in the world, but its wing motion is so rapid that the wings appear to be blurred even when it's hovering as it feeds on a flower's sweet nectar.

A hummingbird can be seen as a symbol of the lesson nature teaches you about focus. To spot the hummingbird, you need to know to which flowers it's paticularly attracted and at what times of day it likes to eat. Then you need to be watchful as you sit and patiently wait for it to appear. Although you may think that you'll be sharp enough to discern the bird the moment it flits into view, if you're doing something else — if you're not focused on the appearance of the hummingbird — you'll miss it.

The *Tao* says, "A green bird darting in the night. Will you be able to see it? Will you be able to catch it?" Chinese wisdom wisely notes that the flight of the hummingbird is rarely missed by those who live in societies where there isn't much of a drive for money or where money has little value; in places where there are no limitations to human effort, friendship, or time; and in locations where no one counts the hours required to make a canoe or weave a basket. In short, the flight of the hummingbird will always be visible to those who live without the constraints of the western world, with its notions of urgency, time frames, budgets, efforts, constraints, and fixed quantities.

There is a Chinese parable in which a wise man talks about moving a mountain in his village, and he explains that it will be accomplished over generations. Rather than cry out, "We've got to get this project finished!" those workers who chose to participate in moving the mountain did so with a smile on their faces. They chose to live in the present moment, focused on the task of moving the mountain, bit by bit. In performing the task, time meant nothing to them, nor did completing the actual goal of moving the mountain. Rather, it was the task itself, and the ability to focus on that task, that became most important to them.

This lesson of focus is echoed by writer Robert Pirsig, who writes about the challenge of mountain climbing: "Mountains should be climbed with as little effort as possible, and without desire. The reality of your own nature should determine the speed. If you become restless, speed up. If you become winded, slow down. You climb the mountain in the equilibrium between restlessness and exhaustion. Then, when you're no longer thinking ahead, each footstep isn't just a means to an end, but a unique event in itself. *This* leaf has jagged edges. *This* rock breaks loose. These are things you should notice. To live only for some future goal is shallow. It is the sides of the mountain which sustain life, not the top."

The mad rush of living — the crush of places to go, people to see, and things to do — and the beepers, alarms, and billboards that determine the direction your life takes can make you forget what it means not only to take time out of your busy schedule to focus on the things that really matter, but to suspend time in the traditional sense so there are no interruptions in your ability to focus on the simple things in life — a hug from a loved one, the wet warmth of your dog's tongue upon your face, a walk through the woods on a spring day, the scent of wild herbs, or the flight of a hummingbird.

There's a natural world of wonders teeming all around you. But these wonders won't come to you; you have to take time to notice them, to pay attention to them, to focus on them. No matter how busy you are, nature implores you to slow down your pace and take time to focus. By becoming more focused on the world around you, you'll feel more alive!

Trust

"Hold your hands out over the earth as over a flame. To all who love her, who open to her the doors of their veins, she gives of her strength, sustaining them with her own measureless tremor of dark life. Touch the earth, love the earth, honour the earth, her plains, her valleys, her hills, and her seas; rest your spirit in her solitary places. For the gifts of life are the earth's and they are given to all, and they are the songs of birds at daybreak, Orion and the Bear, and dawn seen over ocean from the beach."

— American nature writer Henry Beston

In the tapestry of life, the strands of right and wrong and good and bad are interwoven; there's no untangling them. The world contains starvation and abundance, violence and gentleness, harmony and discord in its pattern. To trust that good will always triumph over evil isn't hopeless, but it also isn't realistic. Yet neither is it worthwhile to believe that catastrophe will always strike.

Your trust and faith in the world shouldn't always be shaken because bad things happen to you or to those you love, nor should you begin to feel trust and faith only when good things start to happen to you and your loved ones. Things happen simply because they happen. There's really no cosmic design; oftentimes events are as chancey and unpredictable as a roll of the dice. Or, as English physicist Stephen Hawking once opined, "God not only plays dice with the universe, but sometimes throws them where we can't see them."

Even though, at times, "the odds" appear to be more in the favor of bad fortune rather than good fortune, you can still develop and foster a self-affirming trust and faith in life. You can do this through nature, which every day teaches you what you need to do to develop and strengthen trust in yourself and in the world around you.

The first lesson nature teaches you about trust is that you need to rely upon your experiences. For once you've experienced something, you know it to be true; nothing then ought to be able to persuade you otherwise. So if you hold your hand over a flame once, you don't need a second and third experience to convince you that the flame is hot. It follows as well that if you know, from experience, that it's always darkest before the dawn but that dawn always eventually comes, you'll have trust that troubles will eventually be resolved.

Do you remember the story of the man who thought God had deserted him during a most troubling time because he only saw one set of footprints along the difficult path he had just walked? When he asked God why He wasn't with him when he needed Him the most, God told him that he had only seen one set of footprints because He had been carrying him. Nature similarly carries you when you need to be carried, when you haven't developed trust from your experiences. Nature provides you with a guiding voice of experience that reminds you to trust that all things change, all wounds heal, and all is eased through the passage of time.

Yet you can't benefit from experience without giving yourself the opportunity to learn from your experiences. That means that you not only need to be open to learning all you can about the people, places, and things that happen to cross your path, but that you sometimes need to put yourself in situations where you have to learn. This involves taking risks; the more risks you take, the greater your knowledge base can be. The greater your knowledge base, the more you can trust and the fewer doubts you'll have.

To learn, you can't turn away or run away in fear; you need to overcome your fears. How can you do this? "The answer is very simple," writes spiritualist philosopher Carlos Castaneda. "[You] must not run away. [You] must defy...fear and in spite of it...must take the next step in learning, and the next, and the next. [You] must be fully afraid and yet...must not stop. That is the rule. And the moment will come when...[you] begin to feel sure of [yourself]...intent becomes stronger, learning is no longer a terrifying task." Learning then becomes the basis of trust.

Finally, nature also teaches you that trust comes from a spiritual level of knowing that's gained through your connection with the natural world. To connect with the natural world you first need to cease your vain struggles and lamentations long enough to look away from your personal self. When you can do this, you can take a step back and look objectively at life; chances are you'll realize that, for the most part, your life is probably going quite well. Meditation, too, can give you perceptions of certainty about the natural world and your place in it that can lead to trust. And, finally, so that can spending time alone in nature so you can learn to recognize your physical, emotional, and spiritual kinship with all living things that make the world absolutely yours, absolutely believable, and absolutely as much a part of you as you are a part of it. As Anne Morrow Lindbergh writes: "...And it seemed to me, separated from my own species, that I was nearer to others: the shy willet...the sand piper...the slowly flapping pelicans over my head...the old gull...I felt a kind of impersonal kinship with them and a joy in that kinship. Beauty of earth and sea and air meant more to me. I was in harmony with it, melted into the universe, lost in it, as one is lost in a canticle of praise, swelling from an unknown crowd in a cathedral. 'Praise ye the Lord, all ye fishes of the sea — all ye birds of the air — all ye children of men — Praise ye the Lord!'"

Experience nature, learn from nature, and seek a spiritual connection with nature, and you'll find a source of trust that can lead to inspiration, determination, and personal strength.

Index of Lessons

Photography Credits

All of the photographs that appear within the text of this book are from the Photography Collection of the American Museum of Natural History, and are reprinted courtesy of the Museum's Department of Library Services. The negative numbers refer to the Museum's reference system.

Starfish on Orchard Beach, page 10, negative number 336523 (photograph by Matt Cormons).

Chimpanzee and child, page 18, negative number 337513 (photograph by the American Museum of Natural History).

Ocean dolphins, page 26, negative number 106085.

Model of protozoan, page 32, negative number 321136 (photograph by Boltin).

Mountain lion and black-tail deer, page 41, negative number 337780.

Rabbit tracks, page 46, negative number 102359 (photograph by Mary C. Dickerson).

Beaver brook outlet into Lake Kanohwahke, Bear Mountain, NY, page 55, negative number 260237.

Bear nursing cubs, Yellowstone National Park, page 60, negative number 324695 (photograph by J. E. Haynes).

Wild geese in flight, page 72, negative number 311317 (photograph by Julius Kirschner).

Migrating swallows, page 79, negative number 329634 (photograph by Rota).

Young crows, page 83, negative number 2A4922.

Sand waves at ebb tide, page 89, negative number 102691 (photograph by Mary C. Dickerson).

Roadrunner, page 93, negative number 323268 (photograph by Rota).

Song sparrow, page 98, negative number 125866 (photograph by Rota).

Hawksbill and loggerhead turtles, page 101, negative number 252444.

Beaver, page 109, negative number 332077.

Break in beaver damn, Haverstraw Pond, NY, page 116, negative number 26937 (photograph by W. H. Carr).

Fisher, page 128, negative number 123577 (photograph by Rota).

Young newt, page 134, negative number 335622 (photograph by J. A. L. Cooke).

Grey fox, page 139, negative number 324791 (photograph by Howard Taylor Middleton).

Migrating tree swallows, page 146, negative number 329633 (photograph by Rota).

Tree swallow perched on wild carrots, page 154, negative number 103014.